Curiosit

of

Bedfordshire

A County Guide
to the Unusual

by
Pieter & Rita Boogaart

S.B. Publications

to Plum

Also by Pieter Boogaart: *A272, an Ode to a Road*, Pallas Athene 2000

First published in 2000 by S.B. Publications
c/o 19 Grove Road, Seaford, East Sussex BN25 1TP

ISBN 1 85770 216 6

Maps, photographs and editing by the authors

Front cover: . . . . .Harrold lock-up, p. 44, 87
Title page   . . . . .Elstow black and white, p. 15
Page VI: . . . . .biting dog in Turvey, p. 41
Page VIII: . . . . .Sharnbrook angels, p. 48
Back cover: . . . . .Upper Dean Pub sign, p. VIII
Below: . . . . .Three skulls from Everton church monuments, p. 69

Printed and bound by: MFP Design & Print, Longford Trading Estate, Stretford, Manchester

CONTENTS

III

CONTENTS

CONTENTS

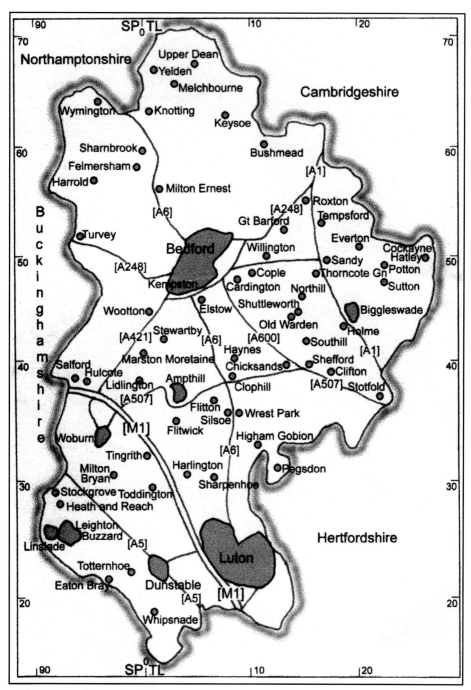

MAP OF BEDFORDSHIRE

Introduction

Writing a book about the curiosities of Bedfordshire is very rewarding, since one gets to see the county from all its attractive angles, meet people, take pictures, do research and what not. On the other hand it is sometimes frustrating, because one cannot include all the curiosities one would like to write about. Some are too private. The old Court manacles on a house in **Shillington** are not visible from the public road any more. The Fishing Temple at **Southill** is a remarkable building, but cannot be visited. There are many similar cases. And we are not even revealing the name of the place where we saw one of the loveliest follies of England, a Palladian bridge. It is in a Bedfordshire back garden, but it must remain private.

Other curios are not included because they are too insignificant, like the gravestones at **Riseley** that seem to have escaped from a graveyard somewhere, or the pumphouses along the A5 at **Battlesden**. In one case we couldn't find out enough: the public footpath through a barn, near the triangular windows at what is called The Jetty in **Hinwick**. Some minor curiosities in the county town are missing from this book simply because they were outclassed by others in Bedford. And another one elsewhere was too well-known, we thought: the Simon and Nellie story about cakes first being boiled and then baked, a graffito in **Leighton Buzzard**'s church.

Churches are difficult anyway. They are a huge source of possible entries for a book like this, but we must restrict ourselves. More is the pity. But there is simply too much that is remarkable. From things outside, like the mausoleum at **Maulden** with its uncertain future, or porches like the one at **Melchbourne** or even a doorway like the one at **Farndish**, to things inside. Old coffin lids at **Cardington** and **Milton Bryan**. Windows like the one for the brothers at **Felmersham**, or for Paxton in **Milton Bryan**. Screens at **Blunham**, **Oakley** and **Odell**. Pews at **Arlesey** and **Melchbourne** or seats along the wall like at **Sundon**. Sanctuary rings like at **Upper Dean**, **Felmersham** and **Turvey**. Decorative elements like the bagpipe player (right) at **Little Staughton**, the rafter owl at **Shelton** or the poppy heads at **Stevington**. Brasses at **Houghton Conquest** among others – too many to mention. A special subject could have been St Christophers, as we saw them at **Bolnhurst**, **Houghton** Conquest and **Shelton**. Or monuments with a story, like the one for Admiral Byng of **Southill**. And how controversial has the modern sculpture of the Madonna been in **Dunstable**? We have seen and marvelled at them all, and many more, but we can't begin to write about them here.

Sometimes a curio can easily be combined with

others, and then we have pages with more than one. Museums also have curios, but they charge an arm and a leg for reproduction of photographs. We had hoped to include at least one lychgate, but none were curious enough (although **Sharnbrook** came close). And there are much sillier reasons why things are not included. The green stones in the church tower of **Husborne Crawley** are peculiar but may not show up green enough. Some curiosities may prove too ephemeral. The sign along a road near **Bletsoe** that tells motorists "beware, free range children and animals" may be gone next year. So may the pubsign in **Upper Dean** that says "customers wanted, no experience required" (back cover). Besides, they have little or no story to tell. In exceptional cases it is the other way round, where there is a story, but no particularly attractive picture can be given. The Duke of Bedford hated seeing neighbours idling and chatting at front doors, so he had houses built with no front doors, and walls between the houses at the back, as at **Milton Bryan**. He also used to change cars when on his way from **Woburn Abbey** to London, since his ancestors used to change horses. Curious and fun, but no picture.

We have arranged the curiosities in groups following routes per region, clockwise starting from Luton, with a variety of subjects and objects. But we can't guarantee that they are all easily accessible. Churches for example are often closed, unfortunately, and it is not always easy to get a key. Sometimes there is an entrance fee for parks and gardens. We have tried to avoid objects that can rarely be seen, but one or two exceptions just had to be made.

We talked to a number of people before we started our investigations for this project, and most of them doubted we would find any curiosities in Bedfordshire. This little book proves them wrong. We have enjoyed travelling round and doing research. General books on Bedfordshire, on its history or geography, have been very useful. Specialised books, on art or follies or whatever, have come in handy. Pevsner of course, *The Buildings of England*. Towns and villages often describe themselves well, and church guides are always a mine of information. The source that we have probably used more than any other is the *Bedfordshire Magazine*, an excellent publication that other counties should be jealous of, but now extinct unfortunately. We have much to be grateful for. But we are most obliged to the Bedfordshire people, too many to mention, who have helped

us. Meeting and working with them has perhaps been the most rewarding experience. We hope that you will enjoy reading the book as much as we have enjoyed writing it.

LUTON 1

OLD HAT

Access:	Between the Tourist Information Centre and the Arndale Shopping Centre.
Map reference:	TL 092 214

The straw-plait industry was probably introduced to this area by Dutch religious refugees, as the Luton Museum teaches us. Nimble little fingers were especially suited for the job of plaiting straw, and children learned the art at a very early age. Dealers went round the cottages and schools and collected the plait, which they sold at markets in various towns.

A major buyer was the straw hat making industry. This used to be a cottage industry as well, but in later times specialised factories were set up in places like **Dunstable**. Hat making became a major source of income. In the second half of the 19th century Luton grew to roughly five times its size because of this industry, which developed its own specialised machinery. Such as hat presses.

Straw hats were gradually replaced by felt hats, but hats for men didn't really last. A vigorous revival of the industry is not very likely. It is all old hat, some people would say. But we do have memorials.

The nicest one is right opposite one of the former hat factories in the centre of Luton, now the Artezium arts and media centre. This hydraulic hat press, as the plaque explains, used to give the hats a smooth finish and the straw a fine lustre. Freshly painted, and surrounded by a bed of flowers, it makes a pretty picture.

Luton TIC at the nearby railway station has information on a few special 'Hat Trails'.

LUTON 2

A BUILDING IN A BUILDING

Access:	Church in town centre, central ring road S.
Map reference:	TL 095 212

The church tower of **Barton-le-Clay** is chequer work of flint and stone, with a blue clock face beautifully contrasting. If you like that sort of thing, go to Luton. St. Mary's is chequered all over with stone battlements, well restored, and visible from all sides on a green churchyard. And it is large; the largest of the county.

So large, that a building inside, over 10 feet high, doesn't seem out of size. It is a unique octagonal baptistery, a white stone canopy over the dark Purbeck marble font. Both date from the early 14thC. The exuberant floral decorations of the gables are matched by a huge central boss inside with a lion and a dragon in foliage.

St. Mary's boasts a number of other points of interest. Famous is the Wenlock Chapel of 1461, separated from the chancel by a stone screen with two tombs and a staircase to the rood screen. On the chapel side the coat of arms is crowned by a three-tier bundle of feathers, the panache, a predecessor of a crest.

The choir stalls have armrests sculpted into birds and beast. One looks like a dodo, but in the 15thC this animal was only dreamed of, not discovered yet. More heads and grotesque faces are to be spotted high up near the roofs.

Behind the iron grill on the right in the sanctuary is a narrow chapel for lepers to attend mass without contaminating the clergy. It is entered from the churchyard through a little door.

Even today this church adds to its treasures, with modern stained glass windows and colourful new hassocks. And behind the baptistery you can find what must be the latest brass: it shows the portrait of a verger who died in 1960.

LUTON 3

THE MONKS AND THE DEVIL

Access:	N of and near town centre, left off A6.
Map reference:	TL 086 223

Luton has some re-markably richly deco-rated buildings. The present Luton Museum and Art Gallery in Wardown Park was a private house of 1875 with terracotta portraits of distinguished Victo-rians on the porch. Also very good are the two watertowers. The octag-onal one on Hart Hill, built 1900, looks like a fairy castle tower with a pagoda hat. The one of 1901 on West Hill Road is a more stur-dy square Arts and Crafts building with stone balconies and a wide pyramidal roof, sup-ported by giant sculpted winged beasts.

In Lansdown Road there are two fine Arts and Crafts houses of note. No 22 is worth studying in detail. With its strangely curved roofs it hides the date 1927 in the richly carved woodwork. Foliage, heads, emblems and shields are spread over the eaves and beams. Note the long-bearded guards of the attic windows. The front garden is separat-ed from the pavement by two double metal gates, together pictur-ing a quiet landscape with monks fishing and contemplating.

Similar woodwork and glazing we can see on No 4. A cheeky devil's head on top of the attic window on the side of the house startles the trespasser.

LUTON 4

SOMERIES

Access:	On the B653 halfway between Harpenden and Luton turn right at New Mill End / sewage works, 1 m., then left and immediately left again, 1 m.
Map reference:	TL 119 202

The only still standing remains of a Bedfordshire castle are to be found near Luton airport. There was an earlier castle by the name of Someries here, but the red walls we see now probably date from about 1500. They are only a small part of the whole, i.e. the gatehouse and the chapel. The rest of the castle and its earlier version can be detected in the unevenness of the ground in the immediate vicinity. What we have here is some beautiful old brickwork. This must be one of the oldest brick buildings in Britain.

The technique of building with bricks is very old. Sun-dried bricks (called adobe) were used as early as seven thousand years ago. Later bricks were fired in kilns, and they were better. The Romans built with thin, tile-shaped bricks. Some examples of their work are still left, but brick building fell into disuse until there were two waves of revival, the first towards the end of the middle ages, and the second roundabout 1600.

Considering that Someries is a very early brick building, it is amazing how confidently the relatively new technique was employed. The gateway shows some lovely arches and decorative elements. The staircase has an elegant handrail carved out of the wall. The squint in the chapel slants smoothly through the bricks.

Gravel or tiny bits of stone are visible in the mortar between the bricks in more places than pure chance or a very rough composition of the mortar would allow, which means that this is a form of strengthening or even decoration. The bricks themselves also have bits of flint or shell baked in sometimes. They are narrow bricks: five courses to the foot.

Perhaps the best form of decoration is the lozenge over the south door. Uneven temperatures in the earlier brick kilns sometimes caused the bricks nearest the fire to get flared. They could become nearly black and vitrified, both headers and stretchers, and the difference in colour was used to create certain patterns in the walls. Later variations of this device were called 'diapers', since the shapes resembled the cloth patterns of the Belgian town Ypres (d'Ypres = diapers).

Opposite the gatehouse is Someries Farm. The novelist Joseph Conrad lived in it for a while (1907-09), but he wasn't very happy here. He suffered from gout, got depressed by his surroundings (this was even before the airport was built), and his great novels hadn't been fully recognised yet.

But one event at least must have perked him up. In 1908 the literary magazine *The English Review* was founded at Someries, by himself and Ford Madox Ford, among others. It marked a new era in literature.

WHIPSNADE 1

TREE CATHEDRAL

Access:	Car park is 150 yards NW of the village green.
Map reference:	TL 008 182

Whipsnade's smaller curiosity is the fact that there are gates at either end of the village. They can be closed at night (they never are), but it looks as if this medieval custom is now only upheld in order to be able to regulate traffic on its way to the zoo. Whipsnade has a larger curiosity as well: the tree cathedral.

At first sight it looks as if the words tree and cathedral couldn't be combined and make sense. A number of years ago in the Netherlands, however, an artist thought of the shape of an existing French cathedral, measured it out on an area of open grass land and planted trees with the key-points of the original building in mind. And now you can walk around in it, and an eerie experience it is. But this had already been done before, slightly differently, in Whipsnade in 1931.

As a memorial to his friends who had died in the Great War Edmund Blyth planted a variety of trees, loosely based on the outlines of Liverpool cathedral. 25 different species of trees on 20 acres. They have now reached maturity. Words like nave, transept, chapel and cloister walk are used to indicate certain areas. Religious services are regularly being held in it. In winter it can look pretty bleak, we are told, but we were there in summer, and we experienced an atmosphere of peacefulness, solemnity and meditation, very much like a cathedral. Yes, we fell for it, but we realise that we saw it at its best. Presumably its maintenance takes as much care and attention as a real building.

WHIPSNADE 2

HOW MANY FEET IS A FOOT?

Access:	SW of Dunstable, below Whipsnade Zoo Park, N of Dagnall.
Map reference:	TL 996 177

Hill figures probably came into existence when natural circumstances like soil creep and weathering caused white patches in the hill chalk, and the local population improved on these by making them look like animals or people. The earliest are over two thousand years old and there is a rich variety of them in the south of England. Most counties have one or two, but Wiltshire for some reason has twelve.

Creating and maintaining a new hill figure is a huge job, and that is why they are rarely made, but on certain occasions people still do it. One such occasion was the opening of the zoo at Whipsnade in 1931.

The White Lion was to serve as a landmark and was completed in 1933. During the war it had to be camouflaged, but otherwise it shines brightly and whitely. It has to be cleaned regularly, but nowadays with weed killers this is less of a job than it used to be. Since the zoo's 50th anniversary in 1981 the lion can be illuminated, for which they use 750 light bulbs.

Some measurements. Nose to tail: 483 feet. Front legs; 103 feet. Back legs: 145 feet. The feet vary. Tail: 13 feet wide. It is best seen from vantage points like Ivinghoe Beacon and from points along the roads near the A4146 - B489 crossing. But the order of magnitude is best appreciated when walking along the edges.

EATON BRAY

FIREHOOKS

Access:	Church in NW of village.
Map reference:	SP 969 207

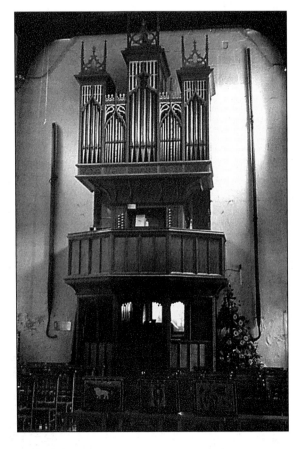

St Mary's church at Eaton Bray has something to offer for everybody. It is built of Totternhoe stone, which can be described as a hard chalk or a soft limestone. It is a lovely building material, but it doesn't weather well, which is why the outside of this church is dull and the whitewashed inside is brilliant.

Real lovers of architecture can rave about the arcades, the eleven rolls in the arches, and the stiff-leaf capitals at the tops of the columns, all of slightly different design. They will notice the 'weeping' chancel (chancel and nave are not as properly aligned as they could be), the modern glass and other details.

People who admire other types of craftsmanship will point at the brasses and the ironwork on the door in the south porch. Others again will admire the embroidery and the splendid work that has been done on the kneelers. The groups of blue, red and green display an enormous variety of subject matters, both religious and secular.

But a curiosity for all visitors must be the two long hooked poles that are hanging on the west wall. They are meant to be used to tear off thatch from buildings that are on fire and they are some twenty feet long. If you have come to this church to see any one of these things, please have a good look at the others.

TOTTERNHOE

DOOLITTLE – DO NOUGHT

Access:	S of Totternhoe, E of Eaton Bray.
Map reference:	SP 990 201

While watermills were introduced by the Romans, windmills were only invented a thousand years later and came to Britain c.1300. There are three main types of windmills. In post-mills, the oldest kind, the whole body revolves around an oak post. Tower-mills are built in brick or stone and only the cap on top turns into the wind. Smock-mills are similar but made of wood, tapering and weatherboarded, looking like a (white) smock.

Bedfordshire has windmills left in **Dunstable**, **Sharnbrook**, **Stanbridge**, **Upper Dean** and **Stevington**. This last one, a postmill of 1770, is probably the finest to have survived. You can get a key from e.g. the Royal George in the village, not far from the cross.

And as for watermills: the only one in Bedfordshire that can be visited is the one on the Ouse at **Bromham**, west of Bedford. Its oldest parts date from 1695, and in summer visitors can get a proper reception and look at various exhibitions before they relax on the adjoining picnic site.

There is one mill we have left for last. This is Doolittle Mill at Totternhoe, a combined wind- and watermill, which in itself is a rare phenomenon. Its name derives from the fact that the watermill didn't get much water from the stream, being high up, and it is no wonder that the milling process had to be supported by a windmill.

But now, from doing little the mill does nought, which is a pity for such a rare industrial relic.

9

DUNSTABLE 1
DEATH KNELLS ON THE KNOLLS

Access:	One mile W from Dunstable centre. Park where the B4541 meets the B489 and start climbing.
Map reference:	TL 006 210

It is a fairly easy climb to this outcrop of the Downs. Most people use the vantage point to enjoy the spectacular views. Very few realise that they are on a cemetery here. Five hillocks are plainly to be seen. Four of them are almost in a straight line, the fifth one is at an angle. They are all barrows: mounds over the remains of the dead. Inside are skeletons or ashes in urns or sacks. Weapons, tools and food were often added to the graves, but these will have gone now: excavated, stolen or decayed.

As a graveyard this area was used for several millennia. There are more than five barrows here really, but the others are less easy to identify. The one that is out of line and has the best position on the spur is probably the oldest, perhaps five thousand years. Its excavation at the end of the 1920s led to a gruesome find. Some thirty skeletons were lying there in rows, their hands all tied behind their backs. Obviously a mass execution, maybe the result of an early Saxon raid on a nearby village. And evidence was found of later occasions when prisoners had been executed and buried at this very site. There may have been a gallows there. It is certainly something one doesn't prefer thinking about, when one has climbed to the top of this knoll, in order to enjoy the view.

DUNSTABLE 2

FIREMARKS

Firemarks are relics of the time when insurance companies had their own fire brigades. They only extinguished the fires of those houses that were insured with them. The houses could be recognised by the companies' individual firemarks, which bore their device and the number of the policy. Of course by the time it had been established which fire brigade was supposed to put out the fire, the house had burned down usually. Which is why we now have a system of local authority fire brigades. Later firemarks didn't bear the policy number and were usually called fireplates.

Bedford Museum displays ten firemarks, all dating from the 18th to the early 19thC. Among them is the one of the Phoenix Assurance Company, whose building is opposite the John Howard statue in St Paul's Square.

There are few firemarks and fireplates left in the village streets of Bedfordshire today.

One is at **Clifton** on the corner of New Road, near the village sign. It is a plate of the company called The Globe and shows Atlas carrying the earth. The other is here in Dunstable, at the so-called Cart Almshouses. It is The Sun, slightly dented, but still shining brightly. Note the decorative effect of the bricks. They are red and blue, and some glazed and burnt bricks nearby create the impression that the firemark was indeed useful.

DUNSTABLE 3

PIOUS PORTAL

Access:	SW of Priory church.
Map reference:	TL 021 219

Over the years we have noticed how often doorways, porches, gateways etc. are left standing or are even rebuilt out of piety for a building that used to be there. The main structures have gone, but these reminders of them stay, often as landscape elements. We call them pious portals and we are always eager to add new items to our collection of documentary material about them. A good example in Bedfordshire is the gateway to the old Britannia Iron Works in the Kempston Road in **Bedford** (p.57).

Another one is here at the main church in Dunstable. Dunstable Priory was probably founded by Henry I in 1131, but the church we see now took more than 150 years to build. Henry VIII's marriage to Catherine of Aragon was annulled here, which eventually led to the establishment of the Church of England. In those days there must have been a prior's house and a gatehouse. The 15thC gateway you can see to the south-west of the church is all that is left of this entrance towards what was a courtyard of the priory. Entering it nowadays is like coming into a pleasant garden that reflects the peace and quiet that must have prevailed in former times. So it's a pious portal in more than one way.

DUNSTABLE 4

REVIVAL OF A QUEEN

> *Access:* In the little shopping precinct on the W side of High Street North.
> *Map reference:* TL 019 219

In the year 1290 Queen Eleanor died. She was the wife and trusted councillor of King Edward I. She went with him on a crusade and there is a story that she saved his life by sucking poison from a dagger wound. She died near Lincoln and her body was taken to London in a funeral procession that stopped at various religious places on the way. At all these places the king later ordered large crosses to be erected, the most famous one being the last one of the route, Charing Cross in London, which was renewed in 1865.

Only three of the original crosses still stand today. Dunstable's Eleanor Cross stood on the major crossroads of the town until 1643, when it was destroyed in the Civil War by Cromwell's soldiers. It was probably situated at the beginning of High Street South, but for some reason a commemorative plaque with three shields is put up on the north-eastern side of the crossroads.

Dunstable gave Queen Eleanor's name to a girls' school. And when the new Eleanor's Cross shopping precinct was created in 1985 (entrance on High Street North, before you get to the Sugar Cone opposite), it was considered appropriate to revive part of the rich history of the town, and a statue of Queen Eleanor was sculpted by Dora Barrett.

Eleanor has a queenly bearing, a subtle crown and two large crosses like arrowslits left out of the protective husk or shroud. Well done Dunstable, on all counts.

LEIGHTON BUZZARD 1

STUDY TO BE QUIET

Access: Near the beginning of North Street, on the left.
Map reference: SP 922 253

There are many attractive almshouses in Bedfordshire. The pair in **Clifton** are charming and so are the ones in **Broom**, to mention but a few. But the almshouses in Leighton Buzzard (by Edward Wilkes, 1633) have the nicest inscriptions. The plaques are all a pleasure to read. Practical, pompous and pious.

"Remove not the ancient landmarke which thy fathers have sett". "Let the brother of the low degree rejoyce in that he is exalted but the rich in that he is made low because as the flower of the grass he shall pass away." "Not unto us o lord, not unto us but unto thy name be the glory of this worke." The latter text is also there in Latin, but other Latin bits have faded. "From the rage of fier and hands of vilence good lord deliver us." "Rob not the poor because he is poor neither oppress the afflicted in the gate for the lord will plead their cause

and spoil the soul of those that spoiled them" obviously dates from the time when 'the afflicted' were not allowed inside the town gates. Our favourite: "Let noe brawlings nor evill communications be betweene you but study to be quiet everyone doing his owne buissines anno dom. 1667", strongly reminiscent of Izaak Walton's *The Complete Angler* (1653), which gained instant popularity.

LEIGHTON BUZZARD 2

NOGGING

> *Access:*   At the beginning of North Street, on the left.
> *Map reference:* SP 922 252

Towns always have a number of peculiarities that people will or will not pay attention to. Leighton Buzzard's market cross is well-known, but while you are there, have a look at the top of the Swan Hotel and see how the name is indicated.

The Black Horse Hotel at the corner of North Street and West Street probably dates from the 17thC. There is nothing very spectacular about it, but the brickwork in the north wall is amusing, to say the least.

Timber-framed houses can date from the middle ages. This style of building was very popular in Britain as well as on the continent. White houses with black oak beams are characteristic, e.g. **Elstow**, p. III. People often built with the materials that were ready at hand. The space between the members of the oak frame used to be filled with wattle-and-daub, a network of sticks and twigs, covered with sticky stuff like mud or clay or even dung. In the 16thC builders in Europe began to replace this infill by bricks, these being sturdier and better fire-resistant. Britain adopted the method and called it 'brick nogging'. Since only small panels between the timbers are covered, usually, there is no need for strict bonding principles. A simple stretcher bond will suffice, but one can often see more playful arrangements, like herringbone patterns. And fortunately, in some cases the bricklayers seem to have gone berserk and we get nogging like we have it here.

There is another example of crazy nogging in **Totternhoe**. Just look for the pub and you'll see it.

LINSLADE 1

OLD AND UGLY

Access: Where the A4146 crosses the railwayline, just N of Linslade.
Map reference: SP 918 261

In 1838 the railway line between London and Birmingham was constructed, and north of Linslade a tunnel had to be built. The north entrance of it was dressed up as if it was a castle. There are in fact three tunnels for four tracks and they have been decorated with battlements and arrowslits, the whole giving the impression of a strong castle wall against a background of green trees. The combination of this medievalism with modern fast intercity trains suddenly spouting out of it is a peculiar sight.

While this railway tunnel may well be the oldest in Britain to sport castellations, it is not unique. Clayton tunnel near Hassocks in West Sussex could be the loveliest, where Linslade is probably the ugliest. There are groups of red bricks in unlikely places, white damp stains, rubbish on the ground, poles and cables, an unsightly shed in the foreground and the whole has a grimy look.

We thought it was simply too ugly to include it in this book. We did take a few photographs, but it is difficult to take a beautiful photograph of an ugly thing. However, when we were in the neighbourhood again late one afternoon, we wanted to give it another chance. And this time, aiming the camera a bit higher, with the sun shining on the trees, it was slightly better. So here it is.

LINSLADE 2

A GAZEBO WITHOUT A VIEW

Access: In Bossington Lane, NE Linslade, at The Lodge.
Map reference: SP 917 259

Gazebo is a funny word, with the stress on the second syllable: 'gazeebo'. It is probably a mixture of the verb 'gaze' and a Latin future tense, indicating that the builder wants to have a lookout point. Gazebos are lower than belvederes or prospect towers, and often elegantly decorated. Sometimes it is just one outside room, and then the meaning is close to that of a summerhouse nowadays.

But gazebos are still supposed to offer a view, and in that respect this one in Linslade fails magnificently. It is surrounded by trees and houses.

It's not the gazebo's fault, however. When it was built, two tiny rooms on top of each other, the situation was quite different. The names of two official walks near here, Greensand Ridge Walk and Grand Union Canal Walk, give a better idea of the type of landscape that could be enjoyed. And otherwise it wouldn't have been thought of by Mr Gordon Cale Thomas, an engineer to the Grand Junction Canal Company at the end of the 19thC and builder of the big house here, The Martins, which has been demolished.

The gazebo is decorated with a beautiful fish that in the past spouted water into a trough, for the horses.

There is an icehouse here as well. Its top used to be visible as a well-built flat brick dome, but it has gone completely underground, so to speak.

HEATH AND REACH

TWO NAMES AND TWO FACES

Access:	On Heath Green, the village green of Heath and Reach.
Map reference:	SP 925 280

Heath and Reach has pleasant and unpleasant aspects. Let's begin with the former. There is a well-designed green with a good number of fine old cottages round it. And in the middle is the combined wellhouse-cum-clocktower.

It dates from 1873 and according to the inscribed stones, which are not really readable any longer, it was a combined effort of the local population and a few philanthropists.

The little building very much looks like a miniature church. Although one can still see part of the mechanisms, the well doesn't function as such any more, but the clock does.

We heard that the village still has an official clockwinder, who gets half a crown or twelve-and-a-half pence per year for his trouble. It's time he got a raise.

And now for the ugly parts. The sandpits north-east of the village are disheartening, and guidebooks agree on the poor quality of St Leonard's church, although it is less easy to say exactly why. The chapel on the green would look a lot better if there were trees in front of it.

But the main eyesore on the green is the electricity pole with its wires. Photographs of the well-and-tower are easily ruined by it.

The fact that we are used to these wires over our heads doesn't make it better. They are ugly, unsafe, and old-fashioned – not to be tolerated in the new millennium, if we may say so.

STOCKGROVE COUNTRY PARK

FIDEM SERVABO

Access:	Ten minutes' walk SW from the car park (one mile N and W from Heath and Reach).
Map reference:	SP 917 291

In the 1930s a new neo-Georgian house was built on the Stockgrove estate for the Danish businessman Michael Kroyer Kielberg (who proved that foreign traders can get knighted in Britain). The house is now a residential school and out of bounds, but the story is that the gateway for the drive up to the house used to have two columns with the coat of arms of Kroyer Kielberg on them, in stone. The motto: Fidem Servabo. These coats of arms were removed from their perches when an ornamental bench was made, by the lake.

The bench offers a view of what is left of the boathouse across the water. This boathouse used to have a pyramidal thatched roof, but that burnt down decades ago. A drawing of it survives, and shows a romantic little building, a proper private centre for boating and swimming for the resident family. The remains, the foundations and some ironwork, are still there.

Stockgrove Country Park was opened to the public in 1972 and performs its function as a quiet and informal recreation area excellently. Small, but full of variety, and some form of wildlife or other always shows up. The bench is a pleasure. Fidem Servabo means: I shall serve the Faith. Take a seat. They also serve who only sit and wait.

MILTON BRYAN

A DRY ICE POND

Access:	Milton Bryan Manor House, on the road parallel to the A4012; private property.
Map reference:	SP 972 304

Icehouses didn't become popular in Britain until the 17thC. Ice was used for making cold confections in the kitchen, for cooling drinks and for storage, but also for medical purposes. Icehouses were built near mansions to provide ice all year round and they were usually located near the water where the ice could be collected in winter. They were often built in or on top of slopes, which had a number of advantages. This way they could form part of the landscape or be combined with garden buildings like temples. A high position was good for drainage and an open position was good against damp. The ice well itself is usually a few yards deep and layers of ice and snow, pounded into a hard mass, alternated with straw. The main trick is to prevent air from circulating. That's why they often had two or three doors for one entrance.

Now let's see how this general introduction compares to a description of Milton Bryan's icehouse, and give some measurements. It fits to a T. Artificial mound, arched entrance, used to have three doors, tunnel of over 4 metres long, egg-shaped well of some 5 metres deep. Near the entrance bay steps lead down into a little dell now, but that used to be a pond filled with water. A dry pond. Milton Bryan Manor House is private, but from the road you can see the mound and the trees in what used to be the pond, if you know where to look.

There used to be some 30 icehouses in Bedfordshire. Most have gone or are in very poor condition. None can be seen inside, normally. The ones at **Shuttleworth**, **Southill** and **Woburn Abbey** can easily be seen from the outside.

TINGRITH

RUBENS

Access:	Village church.
Map reference:	TL 007 324

Tingrith is only a small village, but the church of St. Nicholas houses some unexpected works of art with foreign connections.

William J. Bolton emigrated to the USA and became the first famous glazier, particularly for 49 windows in one church in Brooklyn, New York. In 1999 some experts discovered that four stained glass windows in Tingrith's chancel and one in the tower were designed and made by him between his remigrating in 1848 and his taking orders in 1849; they are his last and only great work in Britain.

In the back of the church there is an oil painting in a gilded frame. It takes some hard staring before the scene is identified as the The Supper at Emmaus (Luke, 24, 29-31), where Christ breaks the bread, and the two disciples recognise him by it. The disciple in the front has his back turned towards us in a strange, startled position, half rising from his chair, his cloak slipping down his left arm, and leaning on the table with his right hand, typical for baroque art. On the right an old woman with a white turban holds a glass of wine, on the left a young man brings in a plate of food.

This composition is recognised as Rubens's. W. Swanenburg, a Dutch engraver, made the first dated engraving after the original in 1611. But that original, probably painted in 1610, is lost. Several copies are known, e.g. in Paris and Madrid. This painting in Tingrith is not mentioned any-where. Unfortunately there are no church archives to prove its provenance. It is believed to be a gift from a Dutch king, some-where in the 19thC. Both Willem I and Willem II spent some time in Britain, but a connection with either Edward or Truman Tanqueray (father and son who between them held the living 1787-1899 - for 112 years) or anyone else in Tingrith has not been discovered. It is highly unlikely that a lost Rubens should turn up in Tingrith, but let's get the painting cleaned first.

TODDINGTON

MISCELLANY

Access:	Toddington church in centre.
	The Manor House is 1 mile NW of the village.
Map reference:	TL 010 289

A Table of Charities Given to the
   Poor of this Parifh
Criftopher Sheriff Given by Will
dated in the year 1611. 40 S L per Ann, to
be given every half Year to Six poor
Widows at 3 S & 4 d each to be paid out
of the Annual Rents of a Houfe and
Pickle now in the Occupation of
William Strange
The Lady Jane Cheney Widow by Will
dated March Ye 7:th 1712. gave a tenement
with a Garden, & little Clofe adioining &
a Cow Common and 20 L per Ann, for
ever to be paid out of the Eftate now
farm'd by Jacob Earl to three poor
Widows or Maids of this Parifh to be
nominated by the Lord of the Manour
and if the Lord of the Manour does not
fill the Vacancy within a Month then
the Rector, Church-Wardens & Overfeers
of the Poor, or any of them have Power
   to fill the Vacancy
Mrs Doroty Aftrey gave 14 S to be paid to
12 poor Widows every Year at Chrifmus
Settled by Indenture of Feoffment dated
Dec.r Ye 23:d 1730. ofDr. Francis Aftrey of
the Parifh of Harlington this Mony is
to be diftributed by the Rector and
Church-Wardens to thofe Poor they
   think moft deferving.
Allfo 25 L. 10 S per Ann. in Lands. & five
Houfes, in the Hands of Truftees.

At the northern end of Toddington's handsome green is the parish church. The first thing one sees on the outside is the 'parvis(e)', a vestry-cum-priest's-house, three storeys high, which is very exceptional, but not particularly attractive. Much nicer is the long row of little animals in the frieze under the battlements. One could argue whether or not the nearby pubs are represented in these curious carvings, but one has to keep in mind that these animals date from the early 16thC, although they are being renewed now. The wyvern, swan and lion are figures of the family of Sir Thomas Cheney, who eventually acquired the local Manor House.

Inside the church there are various attractions such as a double piscina, hatchments, angels and putti, which are all fairly old, and there is also an interesting modern east window with unexpected things like skating children, a Christmas tree and a whale (1948). Our favourite, however, is a simple, large stone tablet on the north wall, because of the detailed way in which it describes who handed out the charities and how. The need to advertise good deeds is nothing modern.

Toddington Manor House is now only part of what it used to be. Most of it was pulled down halfway the 18thC. The old White Horse Inn (1566?) at **Hockliffe**, nearby on the A5 / Watling Street, still has some of the reclaimed carved oak panels hanging outside. They are quite a remarkable sight for motorists that are waiting for the traffic lights. According to the *Victoria History of the Counties of England* two coats of arms can be distinguished. But today they are too much defaced by bird droppings to distinguish anything much, or for us to include a picture here.

What we can show is the inside of the modern little grotto that is behind Toddington Manor. There are relatively few grottoes in Bedfordshire, and this tiny one, in a delightful part of the gardens (which are sometimes open to the public), also doubles as a summerhouse. Garden furniture, fountain, basin and ceiling with countless baby stalactites. Charming.

HULCOTE

WHITE MAGIC

Access:	N of the M1, along the road from Junction 13 W to Salford.
Map reference:	SP 949 383

Owen Rogers had always had an interest in astronomy, and in the 1960s he began to make mirrors and lenses for a telescope. Eventually he built a complete observatory. It is made of plywood, 25 millimetres thick, and painted glaringly white. This is so that the infra-red radiation from the sun reflects off it, and you don't get atmospheric turbulence. The idea is to keep it cool.

In spite of the light of the nearby motorway the observatory can be used for the moon, the stars and the planets, and after the solar eclipse of August 1999 Mr Rogers had a complete series of photographs, taken with his digital electronic camera, which he proudly

showed us on his computer. All heavenly bodies move about in the sky, and when Mr Rogers wants to focus on one, he uses an electric motor on the telescope, complete with a sophisticated correcting device, so that he can automatically follow the object. He made it all himself (25 ft telescope, using a 720 teeth wormwheel etc.).

It is true that he trained as an engineer, but officially he has always been a farmer. He also makes and repairs clocks, and the large building you can see near the farm is a hangar in which he tinkers with aeroplanes with his son. Long may we observe him observe.

Only half a mile away from here is the beautifully situated Hulcote church, with its three-tiered Chernocke family monument.

SALFORD

CAN WE HAVE OUR BELL BACK, PLEASE?

Access:	Village church.
Map reference:	SP 936 392

Salford is a quiet little village with a church that has some interesting features, such as the north porch, made with old beams (one is 13thC), and the bellcote. The church bells used to hang in the tower which formed part of the west nave, but in 1867 William White carried out the alteration in which they got this special place for three bells on the west face of the church.

Bellcotes are rare. This wooden one, with heavy curved crossings, is also peculiar because one bell is missing. Information inside the church reveals that the third bell was stolen a few years ago during repairs to the bellcote. The mind boggles. How does one steal a large church bell that weighs a ton?

Well, these bells do not exactly weigh a ton. Here is some more information. The smaller bell is by James Keene, Woodstock 1628, approximately 3 1/4 cwt. The large bell dates from the mid-15thC and weighs 5 3/4 cwt. We can follow all that, but the next bit of text is tricky. "The bells are supported on timber headstocks in plain bearings, they are hung for swing chiming. Both bells have cast-in staples and retain their canons; they are untuned and have not been turned. The clappers are in poor condition. There is infestation in the upper supporting timbers and the headstock of the larger bell is slightly split." It is very obvious to all readers that some expert has had an expert look and wants to let us know in expert terms.

WOBURN ABBEY 1

A FINE PLACE

Access:	NE of the House, near Chinese Dairy.
Map reference:	SP 967 327

Neither Dr Johnson's jocular definition of a grotto ("a fine place ... for a toad, madam") nor his more serious one ("a cavern made for coolness") applies to the outside grotto at Woburn. Grottoes are supposed to be damp and dark places, half or wholly subterranean, and this one in Woburn's Pleasure Grounds is of the free-standing type. It has a ruined look, which was fashionable at the time it was built, in the 19thC. So it wasn't made with materials that were left over after the rather splendid and elaborate grotto room inside the House was built, as has been suggested, for the inside one was done some 200 years earlier.

Few people have eyes for this outside grotto, which is a pity, but understandable. There are so many things that have a more immediate appeal. Like the Chinese Dairy opposite for example, or indeed the House itself. And there are also more remote delights, such as the Thornery, built by Humphry Repton in 1808. Woburn Abbey and its divers attractions is worth more than a day to enjoy.

And even outside the perimeter some things are worth a second look. A minor curiosity is formed by the buttresses outside the seemingly endless brick wall that surrounds the estate. In the northern corner the material is iron, but made to look like the surrounding brick. It is said that the 11th Duke who rebuilt the wall in 1900 wanted to support the iron works of a friend.

WOBURN ABBEY 2

PARIS HOUSE

Access:	Near the London Entrance of Woburn Abbey, in the far S of the Park.
Map reference:	SP 965 313

Near the London Entrance to Woburn Abbey the drive comes along a house that is strongly reminiscent of 16thC architecture of the Cheshire region. It is not only out of place but out of time as well. For it is a fake, so to speak. It was designed in 1878, by William Cubitt and Son for the International Exhibition of Paris in 1878. The 9th Duke of Bedford (1872-1891) saw it there and fell in love with it. He had the house rebuilt at home, where it became known as Paris House.

For a time it was also known as the 'Tonsil Hospital', when it was used as a hospital by Duchess Mary, the Flying Duchess. Afterwards it was lived in by various people like the pilot who had rescued the Duchess when her plane crashed in the desert, the Queen Mother's brother, General de Gaulle and senior staff members, until in the late 1970s it got the destination it still has today: a restaurant.

Inside there is this dark and carved wood everywhere. Even if it is a fake in a way, Paris House is an exceptionally beautiful building and the Duke did well to save it from having to live out its life in France.

WOBURN

DECEPTIVE APPEARANCES

Access:	Almshouses in N of village.
Map reference:	SP 948 334

The village of Woburn is so pleasing because the houses show elegant 18thC fronts, even if they are older at the back. A few of them have door columns that are curved outwards at the top. Quite unspectacular, but quite nice. Most houses owe their Georgian appearance to the fact that the town had to be largely rebuilt after some fires.

But the 'deceit' is structural. The old school is Elizabethan but doesn't look it. The parish church (a hall church) was built in the 19thC, but in the style of the 12thC. The cobbles in the village centre look quiet and neat, but there are stories about tunnels and cellars underneath, some with wells.

And, to give one more example, at the north-western end of the village are two groups of almshouses, of yellow brick. They were first built by the then Duke of Bedford in 1762 for twelve poor families, but extensively restored in 1850. The stepped gables make them look decidedly Dutch. But they aren't, and nobody seems to know why they were rebuilt in this Dutch style. In 1986 they were modernised into flats for retired parishioners and the whole was renamed Staunton House, since originally they had been built using funds that came from the will of Sir Francis Staunton. Staunton's monument is in the big 1868 chapel with the medieval tower beside it. Sometimes we have no objections at all to being deceived.

AMPTHILL 1

TWINS

Access:	Going W out of Ampthill, before the B530 reaches the A507, turn right for the car park. Take the footpath N and then E.
Map reference:	TL 024 384

Catherine of Aragon stayed at Ampthill Castle at the time when her marriage to Henry VIII was annulled in **Dunstable** (see also Dunstable, p. 12). The castle was already gone when in 1771 Horace Walpole suggested to Lord Ossory that a cross be put up in memory of Queen Catherine. In a letter he indicated what it should look like. "...an authentic form of a cross, of a better appearance than the common run. It must be raised on two or three steps, and if they were octagon, would it not be handsomer? Her arms must be hung like an order upon it. Here is something of my idea. The shield appendant to a collar. We will have some inscription to mark the cause of the erection." Walpole himself wrote a poem for it that is still halfway legible.

It is very rare to find a gothic revival cross as a landscape element. This early, too: 1773. Walpole thought that it should have been bigger. But what was deemed insufficient in size was later compensated in number. A hundred yards away is another cross. This one is a war memorial. The Duke of Bedford had loyally answered a call for help to get more soldiers to fight in the Great War, and he set up a military training camp in Ampthill Park. For those who died this second cross was erected in 1920. Twins; with an age difference of 147 years.

AMPTHILL 2

DUTCH REVENGE

Access:	East of the village centre, off Church Street.
Map reference:	TL 037 383

Whatever people may think of the modern octagonal chapter house that was added to the old church (and there is nothing wrong with it, we think), the building itself displays sufficient reasons for a visit. There are older things like the splendid relief embroidery that dates from the 18thC and there are some modern murals. The modern Rainbow window and the Catherine of Aragon window and other objects as well give the impression that this is a church that is still well attended.

Some fine monuments are to be seen as well, but our favourite is the one with a Dutch cannonball.

It is for Ampthill's most famous son, Richard Nicholls. After Charles I had been executed, Nicholls went into exile and was friends with the Duke of York (later James II). When he took over New Amsterdam from the Dutch in 1664 and became Governor there, he renamed it New York after his friend. With some success, we might add: the name has stuck.

The Dutch had their revenge. Nicholls had another altercation with them and this time it proved fatal to him. At the battle of Sole Bay, off the Suffolk Coast, he was mortally wounded by a Dutch cannonball. The same cannonball that sticks out so ominously from the monument near the altar.

AMPTHILL 3

AN EMBARRASSMENT OF CHOICE

Access:	Town centre (see TIC for map).
Map reference:	TL 034 381

The town centre of Ampthill has a number of curiosities and attractions to offer to the visitor. Too many to mention them all. Some of them remain hidden in private gardens. One is inside the White Hart hotel. It is a wall painting, recently recovered, showing support for the prince of Wales in 1646, at the time of the Civil War. No wonder it was covered up soon after, when allegiances had changed again. It is visible during opening times.

Another curiosity is the early Georgian gazebo in Dunstable Street. It is a quaint triangular brick building of two storeys, with pyramidal roof, now well preserved as a shop.

We would also like to mention The Alameda, a lovely path lined with trees, meant to reflect a Spanish taste in town planning and a relic of the attempts by Lord and Lady Holland to beautify the town in the early 19thC.

But even earlier than that the Earl of Upper Ossory did his bit to improve the town centre, in the 1780s. He created the Market Square and sank a well. He asked Sir William Chambers to design a pump, and here too we have an embarrassment of choice as to what its function is. It is a pump. The obelisk which contains the pump is also meant to indicate the town centre. It serves as a signpost too, for the directions to and the distances from the major surrounding towns are given on its sides. And finally, it is a lamp post. A lampumpost.

FLITWICK

FOUR DIRECTIONS LEADING NOWHERE

Access: In the grounds, quite near the house, of Flitwick Manor, now a hotel.
Map reference: TL 028 341

Flitwick Manor House dates from the 17th and 18th centuries. It wasn't until the late 18thC that one family came to live there and stayed for the next 250 years: Brooks. In all likelihood it was George Brooks, establishing the dynasty, who gave the place the status it kept for so long, complete with a lake, a haha and a folly.

The folly is not a large or elaborate one, and the beauty of it is not immediately apparent. From the house a sort of path leads towards what looks like a broad classical triumphal arch, built in brick, with niches left and right. Then one sees the walls to the side of it and the idea enters the mind that it is perhaps a bridge. Under or over something? Neither. A stone path goes under and a grass path goes over it. The paths do not lead anywhere in particular. And that is not all. The passageway underneath the bridge is a grotto room. That is to say, there is a simple pattern of pebbles everywhere. The other side of the bridge appears to be built in a mildly Gothic style: there are two quatrefoil windows for the grotto room. The whimsical difference in architectural styles and the uselessness of this grotto-bridge make it a modest but charming folly.

LIDLINGTON

CARVINGS

Access:	Opposite village church.
Map reference:	SP 991 388

On the main street through Lidlington, opposite the church, there is a concrete slab in a garden wall with a gosling in relief. It was made by a Mr Gosling as a mark of his name for his property, the old school he converted into housing around 1980.

This school, on the corner opposite Church Street, dates from mid- or late-Victorian times, and may have been founded by the Duke of Bedford. There is no proof of that, but the former school playing field is still owned by the Bedfords. It was used as a primary school until 1977. In 1983 the conversion was ready.

Since then it has been private housing for several families.

But one can still recognize some marks of the old function. The old school bell canopy sits high on the wall. And if you look down from there to the right hand corner of the brick building, you see many scratches on the corner bricks. They are so deep that they must be there for a reason. They are marks of sharpening slate-pencils. As the children were waiting to get into the building they took the opportunity to sharpen their tools on the wall where it was most convenient. That explains why the marks are on different heights: the pupils varied in length. No graffiti in the modern sense, but a well-used pencil-sharpener from the time when children practised writing on slates with a slate-pencil.

STEWARTBY

FLETTON BRICKS

Access:	1. At the roundabout between Stuartby brick works and the village.
	2. At Hanson Bricks main office.
Map reference:	TL 019 424, TL 018 423

The whole of Stewartby is a curiosity. As a model village for the workers in the brick factory it is unique in Bedfordshire, and some aspects are unique for Britain, e.g. the layout of 68 bungalows round a Common Room. It was named after two brothers Stewart, who were directors of what later became the London Brick Company. This firm owed its success largely to the production of so-called fletton bricks. These bricks are made of deep Oxford clay, nicknamed 'the clay that burns', which needs less fuel in the baking, a process first experimented with at the Fletton brick works near Peterborough.

Stewartby village was developed in 1926. Within a decade over 1,500 million bricks were produced per year. Imagine what that meant in terms of storage, transport etc. It was indeed the largest brick factory in the world and some of the figures that historians produce are staggering. After the Second World War the kiln had to be reheated and we were told that this took more than a year. The village got everything a modern community of over two hundred houses could want, including excellent sports facilities: a pavilion, bowling greens, tennis courts and an open air swimming pool. It also had its own social club.

The Stewarts were good employers and they came up with profit sharing and pension schemes. Even today retired workers benefit from them: pensioners' bungalows are rentfree. So it was a successful village for a successful firm. The symbol of the beehive was used on the village hall to indicate the industriousness. The village sign consists of Stewart colours, has thistles as the Scottish national emblem, and represents a structure made of brick. It couldn't be more appropriate.

And what about today? The large clay pits have been developed as the Stewartby Lake Country Park. It had a lovely three-part sculpture somewhere along its north-eastern shores, done in brick, but unfortunately that was smashed by vandals when we saw it in 1999.

In the village itself things look quieter now. Lots of bricks are still produced, but the London Brick Company was succeeded by Hanson Bricks around 1990, and the village sign was renewed.

In the lobby of their main office the visitor can enjoy some remarkable objects. Brick making is depicted in a large, colourful wall painting of 1968 by Francy Walker, opposite the glass entrance doors. An original Sumerian brick with inscriptions is displayed, 4200 years old, from Iraq.

To the right is a relief named Toilet. It is sculpted in shallow relief from a neat piece of flettons brick wall, a favourite technique of the sculptor Walter Ritchie (1919-1997). The figure is imbedded in the wall as it were, and you can see the pattern of the joints throughout the whole piece. It is probably of the same period as the next piece, commissioned by the London Brick Co. Ltd.

This one is on the left wall and is called Street 3, made in 1976. It is roughly the same size, 2'3" high, and of the same material. It is very elegant, and you might not see the curiosity of this piece right away. The figures seem to project from the wall. But this is an optical illusion. They are in hollow relief, like the figures in a signet-ring. You may recognize this if you realise that the daylight comes from the left, but the figures have their light side on the right. It's a sort of trompe l'oeil. Even when you know, it is hard to believe.

MARSTON MORETAINE

THE WORKS OF THE DEVIL

Access:	Church in S of village.
Map reference:	SP 996 414

Marston Moretaine (or Moreteyne as the post office mainteyns) has a detached church tower, just like **Elstow.** Legend has it that the devil once tried to carry away the tower, but dropped it soon as it was too heavy, and leapt away, touching the ground in a field at the Devil's Toenail, or Jump Stone (which is not really worth seeing). Its position and sturdiness suggest that the tower might have been a watch-tower and refuge from the Danes before it became the bell tower for the church built nearby.

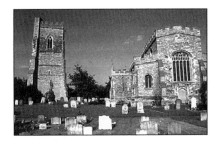

The church is light and mostly whitewashed inside, which makes it easier to view the Doom Painting over the chancel arch. This was painted exceptionally in black and ochre only, with few touches of red, in 1505, but whitewashed at the Reformation, probably around 1547 already. It was only uncovered again in 1969. In Bedfordshire we have not seen another of this size. Peculiar is also that most of the space is taken by graves with the rising dead. To the left they are admitted into the gate of Heavens by St Peter, on the right they are cooked in a cauldron or crammed inside the mouth of hell, another work of the devil. At the top Christ is seated on the rainbow as usual, and by his side are Mary and John the Baptist (with a camel's head still on his camel-hair robe). Much of the paint has flaked off now.

In the chancel of this church you can see three large pre-Raphaelite figures in stained glass by Burne-Jones, for Morris and Co in 1893. Bedfordshire has a number of special

stained glass windows. In **Northill** is a unique heraldic window commissioned by the Grocer's Company in 1664, with much baroque yellow scrollwork, and three lancets with a complete angel orchestra of 1895. The most recent peculiarity is the Tree of Life in the east window of **Totternoe** by John Piper (1970-1), which looks just like a colourful Triffid.

36

WOOTTON

A PAST CURIOSITY

Access:	No access.
Map reference:	TL 00 45

Norman and Valerie Illingworth of Wootton had once worked in the cinema industry in the 1950s. Having read an article in the Guardian about someone who had set up a cinema in his living-room, Norman decided on his retirement to investigate the possibility of starting a 1950s working cinema.

He converted his existing barn into two sections, one being the auditorium with comfortable red seats and the other end as a projection room housing a huge Simplex projector. He managed to obtain a ticket machine which he repaired and installed in the projection area with a small window where customers could be issued with their tickets. On performance nights the front of the barn would be transformed into a glittering entrance with columns and the proud inscription: The Picturedrome. Valerie would usher the patrons in, dressed in usherette costume. It was fun. A bit of glamour.

The infectious enthusiasm of both Norman and Valerie gave great pleasure to a growing number of interested people. The private cinema lasted a few happy years. Too few. In 1998 Norman died of a heart attack. The next year Valerie decided to close down the cinema. It would never capture the same atmosphere as when Norman was there to present it and meet people in his evening suit and give a little introductory talk. So the past has passed. But for a short time the Picturedrome was an excellent curiosity of Wootton life.

KEMPSTON 1

MARKING TIME

Access:	Kempston Church End, W of Kempston turn right off the A5134 towards the Ouse.
	Map reference: TL 015 480

Kempston's Church End is like a tiny village. The church, started by William the Conqueror's niece Judith, retains a rood gallery over the chancel arch inside, with a cross. Rood means cross or crucifix. Holy Rood means that St Mary and St John are standing by, as here.

The cross is symbolically budding like a tree: from death comes life. On the south porch outside there is a bee hole and a 15thC priest's chamber with an external staircase. And also a clock of the scratch-dial variety.

Sundials are a very old device. The principle of them is that a metal style or a stick or even a straight twig (called gnomon) is placed horizontally in the middle of a vertical circle, so that its shadow can indicate the time.

In Saxon times the circle is often subdivided into four main parts, with the principle lines ending in a cross. Later the dials were usually marked in twelve or twenty-four hours. If one of the lines, e.g. the one for 9 a.m., was more deeply scratched than the others or was longer, that meant that the Sunday mass was held at that time.

The basic function of sundials, apart from just indicating what time it was, seems to have been that one could 'read' when to ring the church bells for certain canonical hours, when prayers were due.

KEMPSTON 2

A CLASSICAL BEAUTY

Access: On B531 towards Bedford.
Map reference: TL 039 485

The most elaborate war memorial in Bedfordshire is the one on the Bedford Road in Kempston (or, as some say, on the Kempston Road in Bedford). One column is dedicated to World War I. "to the sacred and glorious memory of the officers, warrant officer, non-commissioned officers and men of the Bedfordshire Regiment who fell in the Great War, this monument has been erected by their comrades and the friends of the regiment." In total 336 officers and 5745 other ranks fell, in the places that are mentioned. The other column gives the places where the men of the Bedfordshire and Hertfordshire Regiments fell in World War II, and was "erected by their comrades and by the men and women living in the counties of Bedfordshire and Hertfordshire."

The monument was "unveiled by Her Majesty Queen Elizabeth, colonel in chief of the regiment, on 11th November 1950." The double door at the back leads into a tiny chapel with stained-glass windows, crescent-shaped, and behind it is a memorial garden.

The whole of the monument, so classical in shape with the trophied corners, manages to convey a taste of the Mediterranean. Even if there are no cypresses in the background, it must make the large colony of Italians in Bedford feel at home.

TURVEY 1

A HERMITAGE?

Access:	E of the village, just beyond Turvey Abbey a footpath goes S. Follow and turn right.
Map reference:	SP 947 523

Turvey Abbey recently became a real abbey, with RC Benedictine nuns and monks. At the end of the back garden in a corner, is a gazebo. Gothick, 4x4 metres, castellated, with pointed windows. It is 1.5 storeys high, with a pyramidal roof, steps leading up to one door at half height. There is a secondary door below. High over the first door is the date 1829 (when the Longuet Higgins family lived there), cut out in stone relief. The secondary door is probably later. Inside, a pious inscription runs round on four beams.

O Lord of hosts; that man is blest
And happy sure is he
That is persuaded in his breast
To trust all times in thee

Maybe this religious text is why Pevsner speaks of a 'so-called chapel', but the appellation sounds wrong. Why a chapel there in this unusual shape? Much more interesting is

what we heard from one of the nuns. They call it a hermitage. At the time when it was built, a landowner who had a summerhouse in his garden sometimes called it a hermitage, following the fashion of wealthy people who used to actually hire somebody to act as a hermit. In other cases there was a doll that played the part. But this building is much too elegant to be a real hermitage.

The nuns also tell the story that the estate manager had it as his office, and used to pay out the workers here. It was supposed to have the advantage of being small enough to make it impossible for people to see what the others were paid. It could indeed be used as an office, but the story is slightly silly, isn't it? No. A gazebo, we think. It has all the distinguishing marks.

TURVEY 2

HEADS ON HELMETS

Access:	Village church.
Map reference:	SP 941 525

Just like many old churches Turvey's All Saints has a number of treasures. Font, sedilia and piscina – all probably 13thC. An impressive early 14thC painting of the Crucifixion. An old weathercock, with the date 1630 cut out in its metal. There are also some brasses, but most of all this church should be noted for the Mordaunt tombs.

One is for John Mordaunt and his wife Edith Latimer (1506). The dog pulling the seam of her gown (p. VI) must signify unfaithfulness. Sir John's neatly combed head rests on his helmet, that is crowned with a screaming or probably biting head (from French 'un homme mordant').

Another John Mordaunt, the first Lord, lies with his wife Elizabeth Vere under a triumphal-arch-like canopy of 1562. Here the head on the helmet is Negroid, with turban and earrings, supposedly a Moor, for the first part of the family name.

With the second Lord John Mordaunt, who died in 1571, this Moor's head is distinctly black. His tomb is a double-decker: He is raised on a platform between his two wives. Note how he balances his legs on his spurs in the straw mat.

Lewis, third Lord Mordaunt (died 1601) and his wife have no effigies on their black tomb, but only a sculpted pall. Lewis was one of the judges who reluctantly sent Mary Queen of Scotts to the block, as he could not but obey his Queen on her demand: "Her head, my Lord - or yours", as popular belief has it. At that moment he must have feared death, as the family name of Mordaunt also suggests (morte-daunt). The head on the coat of arms in his case is clearly a woman's, bare-breasted and turbaned, with long hair.

TURVEY 3

JONAH WAS GAY?

Access:	To be seen from the bridge over the Ouse, west of Turvey.
Map reference:	SP 938 524

'Jonah and his wife' are the names the people of Turvey have given to two statues that are placed on an island in the river Ouse, west of the village. Jonah originally came from Hertfordshire, but was placed in Turvey's mill-stream in 1844 by squire Higgins, who did good work remodelling the village at the time.

Maybe Jonah was called Jonah because he has his knee bent over a fish. The fact that it looks more like a dolphin than a whale is not important of course. Some say that the statue represents fisherman St Peter, but this connection is also tenuous. Tobias would make more sense, but let's not take this too seriously.

More than a hundred years later, in 1953, Jonah was joined by a second statue a few yards away. It had been found in a barn by the then mill-owner, who thought it might be a suitable companion for Jonah.

It was a female figure, as most people seem to agree. The head was missing, but a solution was soon found. Some assorted heads happened to be lying nearby, and a suitable one was chosen. It had a three-cornered hat and a beard, but in spite of his obviously being a man the villagers called him Jonah's wife. They must have had inside information and known that Jonah was gay.

Anyway, we were not too surprised to see that Jonah's wife couldn't be seen through the clinging ivy when we were there. A cover-up?

TURVEY 4

TURVEY STROLL

Access:	Start at village church.
Map reference:	SP 941 525

It sometimes happens that a church door is locked and you can't get a key. It also happens you have to wait. There is no better place to spend an hour walking round than Turvey. Some of its curiosities deserve a page of their own. They have got it. Others are grouped here.

Next to the bridge over the Ouse is the old inn Ye Three Fyshes, of 1624. It has a quaint but appropriate pubsign and displays marks indicating how high the water came on the pub wall at various floods: 1797, 1947, and the highest: 1823, when the whole village must have been inundated.

Turning towards the village, in Newton Lane on the right is Nell's Well under an arch. Or rather: was, for the pump is gone. The water had become suspect by the 1960s and in spite of petitions to keep the well it was finally dismantled. But the plaque is still there.

Turning back and crossing the main road one sees (on the left) one of the reasons why Turvey has the reputation of having half-ecclesiastical buildings. This used to be the coach house for the Manor.

Turvey's lock-up and pound are in May Road. Note the beautiful chimney stacks near the A428 when you come back. They rival the ones on the Henry VII lodge in **Aspley Guise**.

Back at the church first marvel at the enormous Higgins mausoleum (see p. 91) and then read the table of Bequests in the porch. Always good fun.

And finally: have you paid attention to the beautiful ironwork on the door? As good as **Eaton Bray**, and believed to be by the same 13thC craftsman, John of Leighton.

HARROLD

A SIGN OF THE TIMES

Access:	W of village green.
Map reference:	SP 949 569

Harrold is heralded in the south by a narrow bridge. Part of it is medieval. It is lengthened in the south by the causeway over water meadows, which makes the whole an impressive sight. There are more of these causeways in the area, like **Radwell** and **Bromham**, but especially since the recent repairs this one must be the finest.

The centre of Harrold is dominated by the triangular green. In the summer sunshine it is hard to imagine a finer place, with its trees and two old buildings.

One is the lock-up (mentioned under **Silsoe**, p. 87) and the other is the market house. It is an octagonal open affair whose roof with a lantern used to provide shelter for market traders. As such it did a better job than the stone sculpted market crosses that other places used to have, of which the one at **Leighton Buzzard** is a very fine example. This wooden structure in Harrold dates from the early 18thC.

East of the green, at the corner of Brook Lane, we spotted an old road sign fixed to the wall of the Oakley Arms pub. We were told that it originally dated from the 1930s and was recently repainted by the brewery. It is certainly rare to see an old road sign like this in good condition, but it is also a sign of the times that the AA can't or won't tell us more about it.

FELMERSHAM

NAUGHTY BITS

Access:	Village church.
Map reference:	SP 991 579

The church of Saint Mary the Virgin in Felmersham is renowned for its size and its style, Early English mainly. Above the nave arches some carved corbels support shafts that used to hold the old roof. Four of these corbels represent the winged symbols of the evangelists. Another on the south side has the most peculiar drollery we have seen in a Bedfordshire church: a kind of contortionist bending double to lick his or her naughty bits. The present ceiling of the nave is flatter than the original one, and supported by wooden angels.

Between the nave and the chancel is a rood screen that sadly lost its loft in a 19thC restoration. But what is left is a splendid three-bayed, oak screen between the loft arches, painted blue with red edges and gold. Lettering suggests it is given by Richard Kynge and Anette his wife, for whose souls we are bidden to pray. Over the gate in the middle between the tracery we find nine tiny angels in exceptional outfit: they wear short golden feather jump-suits over their naughty bits, till just above the knees. These 15thC angels are more demure than the ones in the baroque style that we later see on many graves. But then in later periods the mood swings towards more chastity again. The celestial angel orchestra in top of the modern east window wear long-sleeved white dresses with their golden wings.

MILTON ERNEST

BREAD IN THE CUPBOARD

Access:	Turn E off the A6.
Map reference:	TL 020 561

Milton Ernest shares its vicar with other parishes, **Pavenham** for one. Pavenham has a Green Man corbel (now painted all white, rendering it indistinguishable as such) and is rightly famous for its wooden panels and pulpit and what not. Dark woodwork of various origins.

But Milton Ernest's All Saints church, apart from a number of other interesting items, also has a wooden attraction. It is alternatively called Dole Board, or Bread Box or Bread Cupboard, and is quite exceptional in that it has survived the ages so well.

It was given to the church by Thomas Rolt in 1729, after his wife Susanna had decided in her will that the poor of the parish should be given bread once a week. "Twelve Two-Penny Loaves", to be placed in this cupboard, especially made for the purpose.

Although the text clearly states that the dole should be given "For Ever", the custom was finally discontinued in 1965, when it was decided that the value of the loaves would be given to the poor through other charities. The bread box is a very charming piece of church furniture, and fortunately the parish keeps it in good condition.

We know of only one other, similar specimen in Bedfordshire: in **Dunstable**'s Priory church. The shelves there near the church door are 18thC too and were made under the instruction of Mrs Jane Cart. They still serve a practical purpose: they are used to store prayer books. Food for the soul, one might say.

WYMINGTON

THOSE LITTLE EXTRAS

Access:	Village church.
Map reference:	SP 955 644

We had come to this church to see the brasses. There are three, the one on the monument being the oldest of Bedfordshire that has been preserved, 1391, of John Curteys the church builder and his wife, under a double canopy. They are interesting to the experts, but nothing extra special for laymen.

On the other hand we found a number of details in and outside the church that we had not come across before. There is a double squint that is practically useless. Some of the pews have extra seats underneath the benches that you can pull out into the aisles. New to us. And very practical at one time, probably.

The mural representing Hell, with a monster swallowing people may not be unique in England, but we haven't met another one in Bedfordshire, and it is well preserved, better than the Judgement day painting. And finally inside there is a fine hanging tabernacle in the Lady's chapel.

The main surprise outside is the eastern side of the church, which is positively castle-like: two towers with castellations and arrowslits and all. The arrowslits are useful to get light on the narrow stairs inside the towers.

Also have a look at the tops of the drain-pipes while you are there. It is a church with lots of little extras, which make it worth a look if you are in the area. No wonder it gets good coverage in Pevsner's *Bedford-shire*.

SHARNBROOK

FOR RICHER, FOR POORER

Access:	Village church.
Map reference:	SP 993 596

Hollingworth Magniac and his wife Helen came to live at Colworth House in Sharnbrook in 1857. He had become rich by the opium trade, was a great collector of renaissance art and a liberal MP, and got a memorial in the church as wel as a mausoleum outside when he died in 1867. His son and heir Charles employed William Burgess to make the designs for both, but they are in very different styles. The tall wall memorial in the Tofte chapel is neo-rococo, with many toddlers with only wings on (p. VIII), wrestling, caressing, draping garlands and holding the family arms between the texts for Hollingworth and Charles and their wives. It looks more French or Italian than British, especially because of the many-coloured marble inlay and the curving iron railings like balconies.

Outside, west of the church, is the family mausoleum that was still used for generations

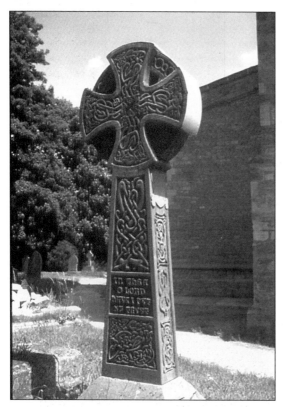

after the Magniacs lost their fortune in 1893. It is in the English style of about 1660, again with many reliefs in coloured marble. The rather pompous stone affair is today protected from the English weather by an inconspicuous wooden canopy.

Hollingworth's daughter Isabel was married to the Rev. Newbolt and when she died in 1914 she got a more simple but elegant memorial, a wooden version of a Celtic High cross.

The humble material is beautifully sculpted in intertwined loops, some with snakes' heads, and a bird. This style was probably chosen to express the zeal of the early Christians in this part of the world as opposed to the worldly ostentatious monuments of her family.

UPPER DEAN

A HUMBLE CHOICE

Access:	The chapel is N of the church, along the road to Lower Dean.
Map reference:	TL 048 679

Upper Dean's church is among the best of Bedfordshire in our recollection. We had come to see the gargoyles, but the feeling of surprise started at the short and lovely leafy lane that led up to the porch, where the door was open. The wooden ceiling with the angels, the alms box, the door within a door, etc. All splendid. But rather than write about yet another church, let us make a choice for more humility and say something about a chapel this time.

The history of Upper Dean's United Reformed Chapel is explained inside. The interior is stark, austere. The wooden furniture has a special style with nice umbrella stands complete with little troughs in the central aisle. Everything looks well-kept as if a multitude of ladies keep it clean, but the services, once a fortnight, are attended by only about a dozen people now. The schoolroom round the back is for Sunday school, but also for services, since the chapel is often felt to be too big.

The style of the building is striking. Good decorated brickwork everywhere and metal columns at the main window. But it has become redundant. Let's look down for a lowly little curio here. On both sides of the porch door are scrapers, for cleaning boots, in their own special little brick housing.

YELDEN

CELTIC QUEEN

Access:	E of village.
Map reference:	TL 014 670

Motte: mound or artificial hill. A motte-and-bailey castle was a sort of fortress or castle introduced by the Normans. They were first built mostly in wood and later in stone. The strongest part was the motte where the lord lived in a tower house or keep. The word bailey is used for the forecourt as well as the external wall, which usually consisted of a palisaded rampart and a ditch. Very often not much more than a dry ditch round a hill is to be seen if these haven't been re-used. There are many remains of motte and bailey castles throughout Britain, but for Bedfordshire we have chosen Yelden. On the one hand because the site here is in a very quiet and remote northern corner, and unusually large. It takes some detective work to spot the one motte, the two baileys and three towers. For amateurs this is an ideal site for speculation. The problem lies of course in the fact that the castle was a ruin in the 14thC already. A second reason to chose this one is that the name of a famous lady may be connected with it. It is said that Boudicca or Boadicea died here. But unfortunately, Yelden is only one of many places that claim relations with Boudicca, because she was the stuff that legends and myths are made of. After gross personal maltreatment by the Romans she led a revolt against them and conquered London and St Albans. Wild revels and human sacrifices accompanied her successes, but eventually she was defeated, and committed suicide. Her grave may be here. Or anywhere, really.

MELCHBOURNE

A FUTURE CURIOSITY?

Access:	From Melchbourne halfway towards Knotting (p.52), on the left.
Map reference:	TL 015 642

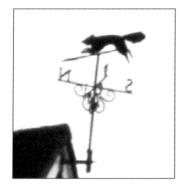

Melchbourne church boasts a porch, a pew and a propeller to make it remarkable, but something that may not last too long as such is more appropriate here: the home of the Oakley Hunt, halfway towards **Knotting**. The office and living quarters were designed as a building with a curious curve. The kennels themselves house some 35 to 40 hounds.

The Oakley Hunt has been well-known for 200 years and has won many prizes. Until the 1960s the strength of the pack didn't vary much: always around 100 (or 50 couples, since hounds are counted in twos). They had 500 square miles available for the hunts, which were held three times a week in winter. It is all a bit less in these days, but the Oakley is still popular in this area and still supported and guided by the Duke of Bedford, who was also one of the founders.

On the other hand we all know that fox-hunting is threatened. The number of people who consider it a cruel blood sport seems to be growing every year. Not that this is the first time that there is opposition. Two hundred years ago the Higgins family at **Turvey** was very much against fox-hunting, and they tried to sabotage it where they could. But this time the forces against fox-hunting have gained more strength, and it looks as though one of the old rural traditions could be lost soon. Jobs will go. But also a host of related things may become obsolete, like maybe pubnames dedicated to the hunt, and weathervanes and such. The examples shown are from Melchbourne itself and **Great Barford** (below).

KNOTTING

BEAUTY AND THE BEAST

Access:	Between Melchbourne and the A6.
Map reference:	TL 003 635

The church looks as if nobody ever has a look at it, inside or out. They don't even tell you where you can get a key, but the windows are clear and low enough to see details inside: the old pews, the lamps, the irregular stones and the iron gates between the nave and the chancel, said to be installed after the rector and the church wardens had been caught enjoying a cock-fight in the chancel.

There is a simple sundial. The octagonal chimney sticking out the roof is more exceptional, and so are the letters carved in the wooden boards in the belfry windows. It reads C.L C.W 17 16, followed by two hearts. Tree trunk stuff rather than on a church tower stuff. A lovers' message? The single-handed clock doesn't work any more, and even the path up to the church is not recognisable as such.

The churchyard cross, with a quatrefoil frieze in its medieval base, has a modern top, which makes it look as if some time ago somebody at least still cared for this remote corner of the world. But otherwise the feeling of quiet loveliness and past rural glory is emphasised and sharply contrasted by the ugly farm buildings on the other side of the road. Beauty and the beast.

KEYSOE

TUMBLEDOWN DICKINS

Access:	Keysoe church, whose vicar holds the key to three churches in this area.
Map reference:	TL 074 625

Inside Keysoe church you can see a strangely crafted font with a French inscription, maybe dating from before 1300. According to the experts it begins with the word Trestin (= all those?) Trestin qui par ici passerez Pour l'ame de Warel priez Que dieu par sa grace Vraie merci li fasse. Amen. But it is difficult to read and verify this.

Much easier and more fun is the inscription of the plaque on the tower outside.

"In Memory of the Mighty hand of the Great God and our Saviour – Jesus Christ, Who Presurved the life of .Wil.m. Dickins Aprl;17th.1718 when he was Pointing the Steepol and Fell From the Rige of the Middel Window in the Spiar Over the South West Pinackel he Dropt Upon the Batelment and their Broaek his Leg and foot and Drove down 2 Long Cope in Stone and so Fell to the Ground with his Neck Upon one Standard of his Chear When the Other End took the Ground Which was the Nearest of Killing him Yet when he See he was Faling Crid Out to his Brother Lord Daniel Wots the Matter Lord Have Mercy Upon me Christ Have Mercy Upon me Lord Jesus Christ Help me But Now Almoust to the Ground   Died Nov.r 29th.1759 Aged 73 Years."

The height from which he fell, halfway the spire, and lived, is impressive, as you can see in the picture. But one cannot help wondering how he had the time to cry out all of that before hitting the ground.

BUSHMEAD

STAR-GAZING FROM A GROTTO

Access:	A private house south of Bushmead Priory, between Colmworth and Little Staughton.
Map reference:	TL 116 584

Bushmead Priory was taken over by the Gery family in 1562 and they have been there ever since. They are a bit vague about their history, but they think that the little tower called the Grotto was built by a William Wade-Gery who was one of a large family then. A number of his brothers and sisters died of tuberculosis, caused by cows' milk. That sad story is told in one of the monuments in the church at **Little Staughton**.

The Grotto was probably built as a summerhouse-cum-observatory towards the end of the 18thC. For a hundred years there was a telescope on the top floor. Nothing too fancy perhaps, but the roof could slide from side to side to enable a view up from the top room.

Around 1900 the building was converted into a house. Or so we were told by William Wade-Gery, who thought that he was the 15th eldest son William in the family and kept repeating that he wasn't too sure of his facts. And better information wasn't to be had.

Why the house, now lived in by one of the estate's officers, is called The Grotto is a mystery to Mr Wade-Gery, he told us, but after having taken a closer look we can safely say that the name is derived from the grotto-like decorations at the back of the building, at ground floor level. They may well be the remnants of a shell grotto.

Isn't it an attractive thought? Grotto or grotto room on the ground floor, tea-room on the first floor (which had large windows then), and observatory on the top floor.

BEDFORD 1

THE MUSIC EXCHANGE

Access:	The Corn Exchange, an 1870s building in St Paul's Square, N.
Map reference:	TL 050 497

The American Glenn Miller was an all-round musician. He played several instruments and was a composer, but became best-known as a band leader, from 1937 onwards. His orchestrations were instantly recognisable for their jazzy sound of saxophones and clarinets. He put 'swing' into dance-music, a style which became much loved, in the USA as well as over here. *Moonlight Serenade*, *Little Brown Jug*, *American Patrol* and the unforgettable *In the Mood*, to name but a few.

From 1941 until his death he conducted military bands, becoming leader of the USA Air Force band, which was often stationed near Bedford and played at the Corn Exchange - Lombardo Hall. Miller stayed at **Milton Ernest** Hall at the time. In 1944 his plane with destination Paris took off from **Tempsford** and disappeared, never to be found again. Miller was forty at the time.

It was only in the year 2000 that somebody came forward with a report on the offloading of bombs in a certain area where no planes were supposed to be flying, but unfortunately there happened to be one, and it was hit. Considering date and time they are pretty sure now that it must have been Miller's plane.

In 1953 a Hollywood-style movie biography was released, '*The Glenn Miller Story*', which contributed greatly to the intensity of his popularity. On the occasion of the fiftieth anniversary of his death a special festival was organised and this bust of a smiling Glenn Miller in uniform was put up on the Corn Exchange.

BEDFORD 2

STREET SCULPTURES

Bedford centre, like any other major town, sports a few oddities that, to paraphrase old Dr Johnson, are worth seeing, but maybe not worth going to see.

In the High Street are a few shop fronts that attract attention. No 57, Dunn & Co, has a neo-Gothic top with two dogs at the ends. Or rather hounds maybe, to reflect the trade of the gunsmith there at the time.

No 49 used to be a jeweller's shop owned by John Bull & Co, and the clock and golden bull are still there, though the bull is a fibre-glass copy of the original wooden one.

In nearby St Paul's Square is the Phoenix to remind us of the insurance company of that name.

Opposite is the John Howard monument which from a distance looks a normal, fitting statue to celebrate the life of a local celebrity. But a closer look reveals some very subtle moulding. It was done by a master of his trade: Sir Alfred Gilbert, who is most famous for his Eros in Piccadilly Circus in London.

The base of this Howard statue is partly Jugendstil, in which masks, held up by babies, are seen to hide other dreamy little baby heads. The graceful design with flowing lines is mystifying, but the innocence and the masks may be symbolic for the famous prison reformer's views.

BEDFORD 3

BRITANNIA IRON WORKS

Access:	Kempston Road (B531), opposite the hospital.
Map reference:	TL 046 491

John Howard (not the prison reformer) founded the Britannia Iron Works in 1813 when he became an ironmonger and started to make all sorts of agricultural implements in Bedford. The chief product was ploughs. The first iron wheel plough was made here, and later, after his sons had taken over in the 1850s, the firm became famous for its steam ploughs. By then they had moved to the Kempston Road.

A London architect, Robert Palgrave, designed all the new buildings there in an Italian style. The plans for the free-standing gateway date from 1859. At the time it was considered sumptuous and described as "the portal to some Sybaritic Castle of indolence, or

some Luxurious place of learning or anything indeed other than a temple of industry". It carried the motto "Whatsoever thy hand findeth to do, do it with thy might", reflecting the Methodist outlook on life of the Howards.

The firm prospered and became internationally famous. In 1864 the Italian general Garribaldi visited the factories and was reported to be most impressed. But later the crisis of 1930 introduced a period of take-overs, and the trade gradually moved away.

All the buildings were eventually pulled down in 1989 except for this proud gateway, which was left standing out of piety for the past, and became a listed building. So here we have an officially recognised 'pious portal' (the term was explained on p. 12).

BEDFORD 4

AN ILL-FATED MILL

Access:	Cardington sluice bridge, in Priory Country Park, near the car park at the Cardington Mill entrance in the SE.
Map reference:	TL 079 489

Priory Country park, south-east of Bedford's centre, covers almost 300 acres and was named for the Augustinian priory that used to be there. It is an area where the modern architecture of some facilities, like the athletics centre and a superstore, tries to live up to the county's motto of being progressive.

The combination of sport, passive recreation and nature works well. The sports include sailing, canoeing (the slalom) and fishing (for which you can get day tickets if you have a licence and meet no fewer than 12 conditions). Some bits of the park are closed to the public to allow nature a chance of undisturbed development. The Visitor Centre contains much information about that and about activities in general.

Few people know where to find the plaque that commemorates the watermill that used to be here (you can see it looking down from the bridge at the Cardington Mill car park). A watermill is not the first building one thinks of in terms of burning down, but to this one it happened twice. It was rebuilt three times according to the plaque, but where accidents and what not failed, the Bedford Corporation succeeded. The watermill is no more.

REBUILT BY S.WHITBREAD ESQ. 1786 - J. SMEATON ENGINEER - WAS DESTROYED BY FIRE DECEMBER 1823 - REBUILT BY W.H.WHITBREAD ESQ. 1824 - AGAIN DESTROYED BY FIRE AUGUST 1840 - AND REBUILT THE SAME YEAR - BY W.H.WHITBREAD ESQ. - AND DEMOLISHED BY THE BEDFORD CORPORATION - NOVEMBER 1936.

CARDINGTON

HANGERS ON

Access:	SE of Bedford and Shortstown, near the A600.
Map reference:	TL 082 468

After the Short brothers (of garden village Shortstown) had started building some military airships at Cardington from 1916 onwards, the future of passenger air travel was thought to lie in airships rather than aeroplanes. Two giant airships, R100 and R101, were built in special hangars. The project was put under undue pressure by the government, and the competition between the two airships was such that too much was tried out too soon. A number of books (like *Slide Rule* by Nevil Shute) and even an exhibition in Cardington church explain about it: no wonder things went wrong. The R101 crashed over France on her maiden voyage in 1930, killing 48 passengers and crew. The country was stunned, national pride was hurt and airship production all but given up.

But these hangars remain. They are landmarks, 180 feet high and 880 feet long; the doors, weighing close to one thousand tons, take half an hour to open. The British Research Establishment owns one. Inside the building they have built houses and flats up to seven stories high, of wood and of concrete, in which they conduct experiments with fire. For instance electric wiring is burnt, and wood, to see how quickly the fire spreads. The other hangar is owned by the MOD, who rent it out. But they are moving away from here, so the future is unclear at the moment. And still the hangars hang on.

Apart from an exhibit about the two airships Cardington church has a few other monuments that are worth seeing, like the black Wedgwood font and the Whitbread memorials. We were also pleased to see the Delft blue plaque near the entrance.

COPLE

SECOND-HAND

> *Access:* Church, village centre.
> *Map reference:* TL 103 485

Cople is only a small village, but it has some remarkable points of interest. One is along the former turnpike road A603: the tollhouse from about 1770, with windows in the sides of the porch. It is rare, since most tollhouses have become victim to subsequent road-widening schemes (the only other Bedfordshire one being at **Bromham,** Stagsden road).

The next curiosity is the parish bier-house, now in a private garden just outside the church wall. It was built at the end of the 19th century, of brick and timbers. The only other bierhouse in Bedfordshire that we saw was at **Keysoe,** opposite the church gate, but Cople's is in better condition.

Last but not least there is a good collection of brasses in the east side of the church, some in the floor, some on tombs or on the wall. Behind the organ there is a display model of the most curious of them: the Cople palimpsest, as it has come to be called. John (d. 1435) and Margaret Launce-lyn's brasses are side by side in the chancel floor. The brass was re-used. The other side was originally the much larger figure of a knight of 1310. His belt and sword for instance are still recognisable at the back of the Launcelyns. The only way the couple would fit in this shape was by turning one of them round, so that Margaret's feet are beside John's head. A model in the church shows how all this was done. Even the inscription plaque was second-hand, by the way: it had been part of John Veal's brass of 1375.

In the isolated church at **Bromham,** under a carpet in the chancel, is another example of an original brass plate (1435) turned over and re-engraved, one hundred years later.

WILLINGTON

BIRDS OF WAR AND PEACE

Access:	(N of) church in W of village.
Map reference:	TL 107 499

Sir John Gostwick (c.1480/90-1545) of Willington became a very important and rich man in Henry VIII's days. He bought the Willington estate in 1529 and displayed his wealth by building a new manor house and the farm buildings, all of stone and unusually handsome. Only the stables and the lofty, stepped gabled dovecote (no fewer than 900 nesting holes in two rooms with ample shutters halfway the roofs) remain. The pigeon eggs could be eaten (a nobleman's privilege) and the birds were often given as presents to nobles and kings. King Henry must have had some when he visited Willington in 1541.

In his young days John Gostwick attended the splendid meeting (called the Field of Cloth of Gold) between Henry VIII and the French King. In the church, also practically rebuilt with Sir John's money, the helmet that he wore there can still be seen

in the Gostwick chapel. Or rather: a replica. It is so special that the original is now in the Tower in London. Its crest (usually the crest refers to the family name) is on top of it, and only two such helmets with their crest intact have survived, we were told (in which case the other one is at **Cople**). Sir John's helmet crest is a fierce red bird with wings half spread, a golden beak with tongue showing, and upright pointed ears. There must have been a kind of wreath or torse between the helmet and the bird, as one can see in the coat of arms on the alabaster tomb of John's descendant Sir William Gostwick. He died in 1615 and lies in effigy on a straw mat under a canopy. At this effigy's stone feet we see the bird again, now bearded, on the wreath, as if it were its nest. Birds of war rather than peace doves.

61

GREAT BARFORD 1

A NEW LEASE OF LIFE

Access:	Near old Barford Bridge, towards the footbridge downstream, SE side of the water.
Map reference:	TL 136 517

Barford owes its name to the ford across the Ouse that goes back to Roman times. The bridge probably dates from the 15thC and was widened in the 19th. There are a few places at the water level from which you can have a good view of how the new brick parapets were built onto the old stone bridge with its seventeen arches. From the 17thC onwards the river was used for transport, in both directions. But between Bedford and the coast the water level drops close to one hundred feet, so there is a need for locks.

Most of the work to make the river navigable and to stimulate trade was done in the early 19thC. Soon, however, the railways came, and transport by road. The lock at Great Barford was allowed to decay. Until, in the mid-1970s, it was decided to give the whole area another lease of life. The work took two years. The river was cleared from rushes, grass was sown and trees were planted. Great care was taken to make the physical aspects of the new lock, weir, footbridge etcetera as unobtrusive as possible. And now it is all useful again, well looked after and very pleasing. The crown on the job-well-done was the gathering together of a few pieces of the old lock winding mechanisms, and putting them up as a relic of the old days. It looks like a modern sculpture.

GREAT BARFORD 2

TWO-AND-A-HALF GATEWAYS AND NO ACCESS

Access:	Along the A421, one mile out of Great Barford to the NE.
Map reference:	TL 138 531

One mile north-east out of Great Barford on the A421 something curious may be seen. There is a gateway on the right-hand side, a bit lower than road level, and therefore not useful any more. Some fanciful brickwork makes it look very nice, but not spectacular. What is curious is that another gateway is built into the wall to the left of it, in relief. Not a real gate, but a fake. The two are not dissimilar. Why this was done is a mystery. To relieve the monotony of the large blank wall? Unlikely. The only explanation one can come up with is that this fake gate may have served as a sort of eyecatcher to Great Barford House, which is on the other side of the road.

In order to find out more about it we went round to the back of the building, where we saw another gateway, like the first one. We were intrigued and slowly moved forward. A variety of dogs began to bark madly and a woman came to see what we wanted. We couldn't make ourselves heard over the barking of the dogs that were obviously out of control, and before we could utter the first sentence to explain our presence, this female person directed us off the premises. And off we went, glad to escape with our lives. Other researchers might be more lucky, but somehow we doubt it.

TEMPSFORD

TOP SECRET

Access:	Along the Roman Road / bridle path N of the road between Tempsford and Everton.
Map reference:	TL 193 526

During the Second World War the RAF had more than 700 airfields all over Britain. Bedfordshire, not far from London and with some relatively flat areas, had more than its fair share, and on detailed maps a number of abandoned airfields can be seen. One of them was at Tempsford, Gibraltar Farm. Employees there all had to sign the official secrets act, and once you worked there you knew you wouldn't be transferred.

Two Special Duties squadrons were based there with mainly two types of planes. Halifax bombers were used not to drop bombs but to fly supplies to the continent, things like clothing, radio equipment, weapons and propaganda leaflets. E.g. at the end of the war food was dropped near Rotterdam, where people went through a 'hunger winter'. Another type of plane that was used was the light Lysander. They could land virtually anywhere and drop off or collect secret agents. It was all night flying, which is why one of the books about it is called *Moon Squadron*.

Gibraltar Farm itself is no longer there, but a barn remains. It was then used for preparing the agents for their missions: kit them out, blacken faces etc. The barn itself bears the signs of all this cloak and dagger stuff: it looks a simple wooden structure, but there is a well-built brick interior, nowadays decorated with plaques and flowers. When we went to have a look, the old runways were being used by people flying model aeroplanes.

ROXTON

CHAPEL ORNÉ

Access:	Near Roxton House, in the middle of the village.
Map reference:	TL 152 544

Cottage orné is an awkward term, half English, half French, the second part related to ornate and ornamented. It is a style of building that tries to imitate the old thatched cottages, often half-timbered or roothouse-like. In the late 18thC - early 19thC this architectural idiom for studied rustic charm was developed for houses and lodges for the gentry, the main difference being that the cottage orné is much larger than its model. We know of only one instance in the whole country where this building style was used for a chapel: the one in Roxton.

It was indeed built at the time when the fashion was at its height, in 1808, by local squire Charles Metcalfe. He also added a lodge for good measure, which is on the other side of the estate, on the A421. The congregational church is T-shaped and consists of three parts, a tree-trunk veranda running right round the building. The church itself is the main part, while two extra rooms form the crossbar. The south side encloses a sort of rustic little outside room. Apart from being quaint, the building looks perfectly clean and healthy, and there is precious little reason why there should be a notice in the porch saying 'all persons entering this building do so at their own risk'. Absolutely gorgeous.

SANDY 1

HE MEASURED TIME

Access: Girtford, a few hundred yards W and S of Sandy's A1 roundabout.
Map reference: TL 163 487

Cycling is not as popular in Great Britain as it is e.g. in the Netherlands. In general 30% of Dutch journeys are by bike. For Britain this is only 2 to 3%, and most of it is done by children. Bedfordshire's varied landscape is very well suited for cycling. No wonder that the sport had its fans around here a hundred years ago. In **Biggleswade** we have Dan Albone and in Sandy there is this memorial garden to Frederick T. Bidlake, 'Biddy' to his friends. He fully deserves this monument.

Bidlake started as a racing cyclist and established over a hundred records when he was young. Later he invented the system of time trials as a way to minimise group racing, since that was sometimes considered dangerous to other unsuspecting road users. He wrote intelligent articles on his sport in many periodicals, founded the Road Racing Council, was a cycling representative on government committees, was president of the North Road Cycling Club and became the country's most trusted and honoured time-keeper. He measured time, as the plaque says, and he is in short described as "an untiring worker for cyclists". After his death in 1933 a National Memorial Fund was started to create this roadside garden, with a sundial measuring time. May it be timeless.

SANDY 2

WILLOW PATTERN

> *Access:* At Sandye Place school, between the church and the river Ivel Weir.
> *Map reference:* TL 173 489

In the better dinner-service shops one can find china with the willow-pattern, still popular more than two hundred years after its first appearance. Today even placemats and napkins show the blue design, probably engraved for the first time by Thomas Minton in 1780, and adopted in many variations in chinaware.

The colour and the style are from China, but adapted in a European way. The scene is a chinoiserie (not really Chinese, but our image of Chinese), depicting a famous love story that was invented here, not in China. You can read the story in short on the plate.

In the gardens of Sandy Place one can still see a peculiar, Chinese style dovecote. It was modelled on the willow pattern pavilion around 1900 and is the only remnant of a complete landscape here, with a Chinese bridge, a boathouse, fence and of course the willow. **Wrest Park** has a similar arrangement (p. 88, 98); and there it is mainly the willow that is missing.

A Mandarin (living in the two-story house on the right, with a pavilion, an orange- and a peach tree) had only one daughter and she fell in love with the secretary. The father disapproved of a possible match. The secretary was expelled, the garden fenced off (foreground) to keep the daughter inside. She often stood under a willow at the waterfront, the lover living on an island (far left) writing poems for her. The daughter tried to elope with the secretary but was spotted by her father who chased them over the bridge (foreground left) to a rough island with gardener's cottage. And he would have beaten them to death with his whip if not the Gods had come to the rescue and, touched by their love, immortalised them as two turtle-doves flying in the sky together. In some versions they escape by boat and live on the island for some time before meeting their death and metamorphosis. Very appropriately the Sandy pavilion is a dovecote.

EVERTON

CRIMEAN LODGE

Access:	From Sandy to Everton, S of Hazells Hall.
Map reference:	TL 189 494

Hazells Hall between Everton and Sandy has been converted into flats, but was almost continually lived in by the Pym family since the mid-eighteenth century. The name was also spelt Hasells and Hassells in the past, but the present Sir Francis Pym got tired of people mispronouncing the name of his ancestral place, making it sound like house of troubles, so now it is Hazells.

Both Humphry Repton and Sir Geoffrey Jellicoe, two hundred years later, worked for the same family here. But in the second half of the 19thC the house was rented, first to Thomas de la Rue, a playing cards manufacturer and money printer, and later to General Pearson. Pearson had military connections and that is why for a long time it was thought that it was he who had the Crimean Lodge, an army hut used by the British in the Crimean War, brought over to England. But a few years ago, during rethatching, a telegram was found in the roof, addressed to Thomas de la Rue, and saying that the hut had been delivered in prefabricated form and could he please collect it from Sandy railway station.

It is a lovely little building, the walls made of wood lined with canvas inside, and it fits well in the tradition of thatched lodges. But the best part about it, perhaps, is that from material that was left over when they put the lodge together, a tiny little shed was built beside it.

POTTON 1

SKULLS AND OTHER SYMBOLS

Access:	Church, E end of village.
Map reference:	TL 229 495

In some places in Potton, notably opposite the church, one can still see herringbone sandstone walling, as typical for Potton as the multitude of sculpted headstones in its churchyard. Some of the earlier gravestones are a bit crude, but there are many fine specimens from 1690 onwards. A wide variety of images is used, and still recognisable. The earliest have scrolled shoulders, some-times with a skull in between, an obvious memento mori. The skull can be replaced by a cherub, symbolic of the departure of the soul, with little wings along the ears, or draped under the chin like a collar. Drapery or skulls can replace the scrolls, as well as other symbols of mortality, like hour-glasses, extinguished candles and torches. Potton also has several headstones with twin weeping angels, wiping their eyes with drapery of a baldachin, and holding flowers or torches. The angel of death was popu-lar too, blowing a trumpet and waving a palm while flying to heaven with clouds of cherubs around. Gradually more and more classical details like urns, columns, gar-lands and shields, drapery, obelisks, palms and flowers took over the scene, the reliefs got shallower and the headstones duller and more alike, and without skulls. But it still is an unsurpassed collection.

The skulls reminded us of the 18thC ones we had seen in **Everton** church, nearby, not on headstones, but as pendants to wall monuments in the church. No lower jaws, different seams on top (p. II). Drooping wings, collar wings, and a third one, with drapery instead of wings, is fixed to the wall by cords through the eye sockets. Ugh!

POTTON 2

TRANSPORTS OF JOY

Access:	Potton S, behind houses W of the B1040.
Map reference:	TL 220 489

All manners of transport have left their mark on the Bedfordshire landscape. And they still do. A village like **Cranfield** is inconceivable without its airfield. North-west of **Millbrook** is the large Vehicle Proving Ground for motorcars, with a diameter of one kilometre. At **Old Warden** and **Stondon** are collections of all types of vehicles on show. There are monuments for waterways and monuments for cyclists. But one of the more romantic means of transport is the train. And that too has seen support from enthusiasts, near Potton for instance.

West of Potton, at Deepdale on the road to Sandy, where there used to be a railway track, is a pub that has retained all sorts of memorabilia. Nothing very spectacular, but worth a visit for those who are into that sort of thing. Going towards Potton from here one recognises the old railway station on the left. In the south of Potton, behind some houses along the B1040 to Biggleswade, is another relic: an old locomotive shed.

It was built for the railway line that used to run between Potton and Sandy, a private line paid for by Captain William Peel of Sandy Lodge. Peel, son of the P.M., died in 1858. The line was hardly ever used, but operational in the five years between 1857 and 1862. Again, there is nothing spectacular about this shed (and Potton's market place is much more attractive), but it is one with a history.

COCKAYNE HATLEY 1

THE LIVING AND THE DEAD

Access:	Church, W of the village.
Map reference:	TL 256 497

St. Bernardus (1090-1153) was noted for his repudiation of decoration, particularly devils, monsters and trivialities in churches, because he thought it would distract the pious from praying and cost money better spent on the poor. How inappropriate to find Bernard in the choir with a laughing devil on a chain! He is part of the very richly carved wooden panels and choir stalls that are from the Belgian abbey of Oignies (and not of Aulne, as was recently discovered), dating 1689, and re-erected by Henry Cockayne Cust in 1826.

Maybe the devil is Tytinyllus, notorious for distracting praying priests, but now kept in check by St. Bernardus.

Most visitors to Cockayne Hatley's churchyard come to see the Art Nouveau grave of 5-year-old Margaret Henly, as she is acclaimed to be the source of the name Wendy in *Peter Pan*, whose author was a friend of her father's (friend being pronounced as 'fwendy' by the child).

But since August 1998 a new memorial attracts attention too: a smooth slate plane wing tip with beautifully carved lettering. It was erected to commemorate the airmen who died in a plane crash in nearby Potton Wood on 18 September 1945, but the survivors are mentioned too, as well as the dog Bitsa. Seven men and the dog crowded the brand new Liberator plane with only two seats, to get to know the machine and practise a landing on only two engines. They failed, and four died. Bitsa guided the villagers to the survivors.

COCKAYNE HATLEY 2

THE WATER ELEVATOR

> *Access:* In the front garden of Well Cottage, the first house on the right.
> *Map reference:* TL 259 496

The first house on the right in Cockayne Hatley dates from 1675 and is called Well House, because the village well was right next to it. It is not used as such any longer, but the water pump is still there. The inscription on it reads: SAFETY WATER ELEVATOR, C. C. DUNSTABLE. Under the helmet-shaped top is a system of gears and sprockets, which could drive a chain. A series of little pans, fastened to the chain, went down one hole, scooped up water and came up again through another hole and at the top they were emptied and the water collected in a sort of upside-down umbrella and led to the spout. The principle is the same as one can see for instance in Egypt, where these simple machines are centuries old and made of wood, but here it is done much neater and with more durable materials.

Two old ladies used to live here in this house for decades before the present occupants took over and called it Well House. They told their successors that they had used the well themselves until the mid 1930s. They had to turn the wheel twenty-six times before the water came up. The other villagers used to pay six pennies per year for the use of it. But no longer. Water comes from taps.

The water elevator is idle now. Not much is known about this little machine. Record offices can't provide information about the design or its popularity, and the firm that made it is no longer extant. But it remains a rare and lovely example of Victorian workmanship.

SUTTON

CHOICES

Access:	Near church, W end of village.
Map reference:	TL 221 474

Sutton is an elongated village, on two sides of the Potton Brook, which later flows into the Ivel. Since there never was an east-west route of importance there, it is hard to see why a stone bridge was considered necessary as early as the middle ages. Only the villagers themselves can have felt the need for a bridge, and perhaps this limited use explains why the bridge is so narrow. Being just wide enough to take a loaded packhorse it is called a packhorse bridge. Not that the river is deep. Nowadays you can cross it driving through the water alongside of it and cars still use this ford, the only official one left in Bedfordshire.

Local historians seem to disagree about the bridge. It is variously described as 15thC and 14thC, built of sandstone, limestone and ironstone. And, as I said, even its very existence is a bit of a mystery. But it is a romantic spot all right.

The church nearby has a wonderful barrel organ, still working, and a monument attributed to Grinling Gibbons. Again the experts seem to disagree. And you can get the key to the church from two nearby cottages. Sutton likes to give people a choice.

HOLME

JORDANS JESUS

Access: At the bridge over the river Ivel, E of Broom.
Map reference: TL 185 430

At home on the continent we buy Jordans breakfast cereals. Jordans, for flour and feed milling, was started at Holme Mills in 1855. It still is a family business, after the other 400 flour mills of 1855 Bedfordshire have all gone. The Mill is situated at a lock in the river. Seeing the narrow lock now, with its wildly frothing water, it is hard to imagine that this was part of a major waterway once. Wheat and coal and many other things used to be brought here by boats and barges up the rivers Ivel and Ouse, on the route between King's Lynn and Shefford.

The present oldest Mr Jordan in the firm took over from his grandfather in 1960. He used

to be a pilot as well for a long time, for Shuttleworth and for acrobatic flying at air shows. Now he is too old for that sort of thing, but he did tell us about the Jordans Jesus. Or rather, what is left of it.

This bust of Jesus (in itself a rare phenomenon since Jesus is almost always portrayed full length, or only the head is done) was sculpted by an Italian prisoner of war. Nobody remembers his name, but around 1943 he worked in the flour mill. The bust is built of sandstone, faced with cement that has crumbled away now a good deal because of the weather, and when we first saw it there on the grassy bit near the lock we had no idea what it was supposed to be.

It needs a new coat of cement and some sculpting, which it may yet get from Mr Jordans. Some face-saving is in order.

BIGGLESWADE 1

WATER WORKS

Access:	West of the A1, nearer to Biggleswade than to Stotfold. Inside closed to the public.
Map reference:	TL 211 417

Newspring Pumphouse was built over a well in 1906. Three pumps bring up almost two million cubic metres per year. The quality of the water is fairly good, but of course it needs treatment, in the filter house behind the 'castle'. Iron is removed and extra air, chlorine and fluoride are added before it is conveyed to the reservoir and watertower, a mile to the south. A relatively harmless procedure, one should think. Why then the building looks like a castle is a bit of a mystery. Pride, presumably.

There are some plaques on the walls inside, with pompous texts. "The Biggleswade Water Board desire to record on this tablet the sinking of a well beneath this spot, whence a copious supply of pure water is conveyed over a wide area to a large population." Etc. But there are a lot of ominous warnings outside, on loud yellow and red signs. "All manholes, chambers and tanks are designated confined spaces. Confined spaces requiring routine entry are labelled to define category procedures for entry." "If the confined space does not have a category sign it is not a routine entry. Contact your supervisor for guidance on non-routine entries." Et cetera

The excited tone of the warnings suggest that it is a very wise decision to have the building look impregnable. Local authorities couldn't tell us how many unsuspecting workers have been killed here, but considering the severity of the texts one would think that there must have been dozens of casualties in the course of the years. A killer castle?

BIGGLESWADE 2

A THOROUGH GOOD FELLOW

Access: Market place in town centre.
Map reference: TL 193 443

In 1997 the town centre of Biggleswade was renovated to some extent and among the new items were a few bicycle stands in the shape of bicycles. Bicycles are big in Biggleswade. There is a great tradition of cycling here. Not least because of Dan Albone (1860-1906), about whom a book appeared in 1990: *A Thorough Good Fellow* by Kathy Hindle and Lee Irvine.

Albone was an enthusiast and an inventor. Cycling was in its infancy in those days and Dan showed his affinity by designing a new type of bicycle when he was only thirteen. In the outhouses of his parents' pub that later became his own house, he started to build bicycles and by 1881 the Ivel Cycle Works were firmly established. They made bicycles, tricycles and cross-frame tandem tricycles for instance, and safety bikes especially for ladies. Later, towards the turn of the century Albone branched out into making motor cars and he invented the tractor. The Ivel Armoured car came, and the Ivel Potato Planter. And all this time he won many prizes in cycle racing.

Biggleswade has honoured its famous son with a memorial picnic area on the banks of the river Ivel, and honours the cycling tradition by providing these special bicycle stands. A thorough good town.

SOUTHILL

TOP DOGS

Access:	Behind Southill Park House; garden sometimes open in National Gardens Scheme.
Map reference:	TL 144 420

Coade stone is an artificial stone, invented in the 1720s and later produced by the firm of Mrs Coade from 1769 onwards. The factory closed in 1840 and the formula was subsequently lost, but later analysis showed that it consisted of sand, ground stoneware and china clay, all mixed and fired in a kiln. It turned out to be weatherproof. For a few decades it was popular for decorative elements, objects like statues and even for light buildings.

At Southill Park we see it used in the pedestal of the drinking-trough-cum-monument to Jock, the dog of Lady Whitbread, daughter-in-law of the founder of the brewery. It is an exquisite and very endearing little 18thC monument by George Gerrard, who was an expert sculptor of animals. The gardens are open once a year in the National Gardens Scheme.

Another monument to a dog is more readily accessible, although you are not supposed to come too close. It is in the shape of a little rotunda with a wrought-iron cupola on top, and lies just off the route through the Park round **Woburn Abbey**. It was commissioned by the Flying Duchess after her pekinese Che Foo (or Wuzzy) died in 1916, and has lines on a pedestal, by Byron among others. Wuzzy used to lie there in bronze, but he is missing. His mistress also went missing. On 22 March 1937 she took off with her aeroplane and was never seen again.

OLD WARDEN 1

DOUBLE VISION 1

Access:	Opposite the well between the village High Street and one entrance to Shuttleworth Agricultural College.
Map reference:	TL 139 441

In 1998 Old Warden got a new village sign, done by G. Mould, woodcarver. Its two sides give his vision of the two faces of the community: the village itself and the Shuttleworth Estate with the Park.

The village represents most people's idea of ideally English. In the past there was a time when its people were required to wear uniforms of hats and red cloaks, to fit with the colour on the mostly 19thC houses.

And nowadays a show of cottages is left, three different water pumps, and a church which is well worth a visit because of its exuberant woodwork. You will find it closed, however, with the key in **Upper Caldicote**, two miles north-east of here. But it's hard to blame them. A note tells you that there had been 85 thefts in 2 years' time.

There are also some attractions quite near the village. The railway tunnel to the west is not worth seeing in itself, but the views towards the Cardington hangars are fine. Closer to the village, and also to the west of it, is a property of the Landmark Trust, the Old Abbey. Inside as well as outside it is quite a remarkable building.

The 'village side' of the village sign also shows a tree with a skirt – a straw canopy over a bench. This tree is to be found not far from the famous Swiss Cottage in the old Park of the Shuttleworth estate.

OLD WARDEN 2

DOUBLE VISION 2

Access:	Opposite a well between the village High Street and one entrance to Shuttleworth Agricultural College.
Map reference:	TL 139 441

The other side of the village sign refers to the two important families that owned the estate, the Ongleys and the Shuttleworths. Both are gone now. The main House is an agricultural college today, and the Park is quickly becoming a tourist attraction. That is to say, the part of it that is called Swiss Garden is becoming popular.

It was laid out by Lord Ongley in the early 19thC, was neglected, but has been done up and is a gorgeous display of garden architecture even in mid-winter. A variety of buildings, bridges, ponds, paths etc. awaits the visitor. Outside this area in the larger Park is Queen Anne's Summerhouse.

Old Warden is well-known to most people as the home of the **Shuttleworth** collection of vintage aeroplanes. It was started by Richard Shuttleworth when he bought a De Haviland Hermes Moth in 1932. This machine is still on show together with later planes and other vehicles. The flying days, which are held regularly in summer, bring lots of enthusiasts to Old Warden. Richard Shuttleworth was killed in action over France in 1940, but the collection is still expanding.

The Shuttleworth estate had its own cottages for the workers. The striking and colourful examples between Cople and Northill were built c.1790, but the extensions at the back date from some 20 years ago. The village washerwoman had a washhouse here.

NORTHILL

SINGLE-HANDED

Access:	Village church.
Map reference:	TL 149 466

A number of church towers, especially in northern Bedfordshire, have clocks with only one hand. But none of them is better in its place than the one at Northill. It was probably made by the king of English clockmakers himself, Thomas Tompion, who, in 1639, was born in this parish less than a mile away, at Ickwell, the hamlet that seems to consist of a maypole and a cricket green.

After he had worked with his father for a time (his father's name is on the bier in the church as the village blacksmith), Thomas Tompion went to London and learned the trade of a clock- and watchmaker. He soon developed into the best watchmaker of his time in England, constructing the first spring-balance watch to the design of Robert Hooke, in 1675. That watch was given to Charles II, and Tompion later made more watches for Royalty and more clocks for famous buildings. He became Master of the Clockmakers Company and is honoured as such on the memorial tablet at the back of Northill church. But Northill is not the place where he was buried. The national importance of this son of Bedfordshire was recognised when he was laid to rest in Westminster Abbey in London.

Realising that his father put him on the track of fine craftsmanship, one can't say that Thomas Tompion did it all single-handedly, but many of his clocks, single-handed or not, still indicate time perfectly, after 300 years.

THORNCOTE GREEN

HAPPY LANDING

Access:	Less than two miles SW of Sandy, N of Northill. Weekend visits by prior appointment only.
Map reference:	TL 152 475

Going from Northill to Sandy the unsuspecting tourist is startled to see an aeroplane in the fields at Thorncote Green. There is no airfield here. Curious, to say the least. A crash? It looks broken. The wings are loose. But no, on further investigation it appears that the dismemberment is deliberate, and there are large sheds nearby. In fact the plane is taken good care of.

It is a Vickers Viscount F-BGNR and was used by Air France. Its maiden flight was in 1954 and it served for almost twenty years. The final flight was from Le Bourget near Paris to Perth in Scotland, in October 1973.

For a long time nobody did anything much with it, and then it was acquired by Tim Moore, who has a business here. So the plane has had a happy landing after all. Officially the firm is called Skysport Engineering Ltd., and what Tim and his associates do is simply: tinker with aeroplanes. They restore, make replicas, stock materials et cetera.

A sign on the gate of the property says that one can only visit the place by prior appointment, but no clue is given as to how to make one. With a smile on his face Tim confirms that that is how he wants it. Don't make it too easy on people.

STOTFOLD

CHECKING THE CHEQUERS

Access:	Queen Street - Rook Tree Lane, in SE of village.
Map reference:	TL 221 367

Stotfold used to have a lock-up that at the end of its life served as a toilet to the Strict Baptist chapel. In a way it is remarkable that not more lock-ups have ended up as public lavatories – it seems a logical change of function. Anyway. We do not especially recommend a visit to the local (St Mary's) churchyard, but if you do, look at the tops of some gravestones. The way they are worked open is unusual, but of no consequence. Better is the pub there.

The Chequers dates from halfway the 17thC and got its name in 1799. In 1900, when two maiden sisters were the licensees, there was a rule that no more than three men at a time were allowed in the bar. Apparently there was a threat that if there were more men they would become unruly and take liberties with the sisters, who were confirmed spinsters.

We had been attracted to this pub by its sign. For a sharp-eyed art historian it is clear that the left half of a painting has been used as a model for this sign. The painting dates from about 1500 and is by the Flemish artist Quinten Metsijs. It is called 'the banker and his wife', and the banker is weighing gold coins while his wife looks up from her book. Why the maker of this pubsign used half this painting for his own picture is more than the pub or the brewery could tell us. There is of course a relationship between the words exchequer and chequer board and chequer pattern, but there is no chequer pattern anywhere in the original painting.

CLIFTON

WELL - WAR MEMORIAL

Access:	Between the church and the pond, on crossroads in the N of the village.
Map reference:	TL 164 389

A combination of a war memorial with the village well, as at Clifton, is rare. It so happened that the use for the well ended at about the same time that the need for a war memorial was felt. The well at Clifton had been built by Hugh Miles in 1881. Miles was rich; he had a shop in London's Oxford Street. He used part of his private gardens on the corner here, to give the well a nice and prominent position.

There used to be a spout up high, at gutter height, through the eaves of the roof, for pouring water into vehicles, and another spout lower down. But the well was sealed up in 1921 and turned into a war memorial the next year.

After the Second World War a completely new stone was installed, to inscribe new names. The first stone didn't have the names in the correct alphabetical order, but the second time they got them right. Well, almost.

The striking part of this memorial is the ornate canopy. The woodwork is excellent. Crafty in two ways. If we were to ask people: "Can you see from the canopy in what year the well was built?", we doubt we would get many good answers, perhaps even from the villagers of Clifton. But it is indicated on the left-hand side in the pattern of the wood. See?

CHICKSANDS

OBELISK TRIO

Access:	NW of Chicksands park at Appley Corner, take path SW for first Halifax, then straight on Osborn obelisk. The peace obelisk is in Chicksands.
Map reference:	TL 117 395, TL 097 395, TL 104 407

At Chicksands the Ordnance Survey map indicates two obelisks and a monument, but the monument is an obelisk and the obelisks are monuments. Chicksands itself is MOD property, but there are guided tours to the old Priory there.

The Peace monument near the Priory is also out of bounds for the public normally, and has a complicated history. It was first erected in 1816 by General Sir George Osborn, restored and removed by Sir George Robert Osborn in 1856 and restored and removed again in 1976. First it commemorated the victory over Napoleon and mourned the loss of men involved; later it also mentioned the peace after the Crimean War and nowadays

it also celebrates the friendship between the peoples of Great Britain and the USA, the co-operation between RAF and USAF, the bicentennial of American independence, and the European Architectural Inheritance Year. There is still plenty of room on the fourth side of this obelisk.

The second obelisk mourns the death of Henry John Robert Osborn, 1889, who is praised as a good neighbour and true sportsman.

The least conventional obelisk, also the best reachable one, was erected by Sir George Osborn to commemorate his uncle Lord Halifax, who died in 1771. Obelisk is indeed the best descriptive word for this Gothicky contraption on three plinths. And so we have a fine trio of them here, west of Shefford.

SHEFFORD 1

HAVE FUN AND GET LOST

Access:	SE of Shefford, halfway towards the roundabout where the A600 meets the A507, on the right.
Map reference:	TL 152 381

In 1980 or thereabouts John Brindle had had enough. He had been growing apples for a few years, and the business was a success. And then he found out that it would be better for the environment if he didn't spray them with all sorts of chemical stuff, and the idea appealed to him. He stopped spraying the orchard in order to do his bit for the environment. But unfortunately, as a result he saw a marked decrease in sales. His apples didn't look so nice as the apples of other people who hadn't stopped spraying. They were perfectly good apples and even more wholesome than the sprayed ones, but the customers didn't want to buy them. John's business suffered, and there came a time whe he said to himself: enough is sufficient.

He cut 18 of his apple trees and planted a maze. He had always been fond of mazes, ever since he had gone to see the one at Woburn Abbey, when other children went to Sunday school.

So now there is this maze at Hoo Hill, consisting of Golden Leylandii trees, which are nice-smelling conifers. The design is John's own. Twice a year the maze has to be cut, which takes a week. With a second maze on the way John has become quite addicted to this hobby.

And it is not his only one. He also makes boomerangs. He is very proficient at throwing them away and catching them again when they return. Just wait and see. There may be a day when he can throw a boomerang into the maze and it will end up in the tower in the centre.

SHEFFORD 2

SHEEP FORD

> *Access:*   Near the bridge across the river Flit, N of village centre.
> *Map reference:* TL 142393

Places like Shefford and **Clifton** (and **Old Warden** and **Everton**, to mention a few others) have rightly invested in village signs in the last few years. They are colourful, lively and a good way for the village to say something about itself. They often tell a story.

Shefford obviously was a transport and market town. The sign tells us about the railway line, now dismantled, and the tow barges on the Ivel navigation. And there were rivers to cross, the Flit and the Hitt. In this river landscape there were swans as well, which can be deduced from the fact that there still is a Black Swan and a White Swan pub. The village sign also indicates that there was a ford for sheep. Sheepford became Shefford.

In the middle ages people didn't travel much. It was hard work, travail. And rivers were major obstacles. Primitive ways of dealing with them, before expensive bridges could be built, were putting tree trunks across them or using stepping stones. Roads often aimed for fords, which is why one sometimes sees fords beside bridges, as in **Sutton** (p. 73). Fords for sheep were relatively easy to cross.

Shefford still retains an example of a ford, albeit an unofficial one. Go north from the village centre, past the black iron pump and Porch House, and you will come to a bridge over the Flit. From this bridge you have a view of the ford.

SILSOE

LOCK 'M UP

Access:	At Cage House in Church Road, W of village centre.
Map reference:	TL 081 356

A lock-up is a miniature, provisional prison. Sometimes in the form of a strong-room, as part of an existing building, but also, and more interestingly, as a specially built cell. From the late middle ages until the 19thC they were used to put away people for the night, like a drunk who made a nuisance of himself or a criminal before he could be brought before a magistrate.

Most lock-ups have disappeared over the years. Bedfordshire has a fair number of them left, usually called cages. The one at Silsoe looks very sturdy indeed. Round the back are a slit and small window for ventilation. It dates from 1796 and looks as if it is good for at least another two-hundred years. If you want to see the inside, you can get a key from a nearby cottage. Not that there is much to see, but you can get a good impression of the sense of claustrophobia the village drunks must have experienced when the door was closed and locked behind them.

Another of the more famous free-standing lock-ups in Bedfordshire is near the market house on the green at **Harrold** (p. 44), shown on the cover of this book. It retains its original padlock. Other surviving lock-ups are the square ones at **Clophill** and **Turvey**, both combined with pounds, in which stray animals could be kept. **Blunham**, **Sharnbrook** and **Kensworth** have lock-ups that few people know about, because they are in the back gardens of private houses, usually because the local policeman used to live there. They are all used for storage by the present owners, and are to remain private.

Stocks were another punishment device. They have all disappeared from the streets of Bedfordshire, except for the fake specimen outside the **Bedford** museum.

WREST PARK

FRANCE 1 – ENGLAND 1

Access:	1. Behind the House at the end of the Long Water.
	2. Tucked away in the NW corner of the gardens, behind the orangery.
Map reference:	TL 092 347, TL 088 353

The Earl de Grey himself designed Wrest Park House, and it was built in the mid-1830s. The style is French, and the architecture of the garden, with its parterre, lengthy canal and pavilion at the end of the view, all in a straight line, is mostly French too. A typical display of grandeur in straight lines. But most of the buildings and conceits in the garden are a lot earlier than 1830. They are to be found round the edges of the main design and the atmosphere there is more English than French.

The pavilion, by Thomas Archer, dates from 1711. It is a geometrical baroque building with trompe l'oeil paintings inside. Its pure craftsmanship and position at the end of the Long Water make it into one of the world's most beautiful classical garden buildings.

Most other follies and monuments pale somewhat in comparison with it, but there is still a lot to be enjoyed. Something for every taste, one might say. There is a lot of water in and round the gardens. The orangery was also designed by the Earl de Grey and is French. The Bowling Green House is an early Palladian building. There are various sculptures and monuments, an urn here, a column there. One of the statues, of William III, is made of lead, but painted to look like stone. A Mithraic altar with a curious text, supposedly put up here by a Greek army officer, and some Graeco-Roman altars. There is a Chinese bridge and pavilion (bearing the wyvern, the family emblem) as part of a Willow Pattern arrangement (p. 67, 98).

Wrest Park is an odd mixture. The garden owes much of its attraction to the landscape style. In the beginning of the 18thC a new type of garden architecture began to develop in England. Sir John Vanbrugh reacted to the formal rectilinear French style and designed gardens that looked more like the English landscape. The poet Alexander Pope gave this his philosophical approval, calling upon people to "consult the genius of the place in all". Other sources of inspiration were the experiences of Grand Tourists and popular paintings by Claude, Poussin or Rosa. In harmony with the landscape trees were cut and planted, hills and even villages were moved, lakes were dug out and this "natural" environment was further adorned with buildings of great variety. We find Greek temples as summerhouses and grottoes with classical statues. Ruins, hermitages and monuments, belvederes and eyecatchers. Famous for this style were William Kent, Lancelot 'Capability' Brown and later Humphry Repton. Sir William Chambers advocated outlandish elements like Chinese temples. The 'English' landscape style was also exported to the continent.

The most typically English example of this landscape style in the gardens at Wrest is the Bathhouse, behind the Orangery. The word bathhouse as such should not be taken too seriously, however. The building has been attributed to Capability Brown, but was probably designed by Edward Stevens in 1770 for Jemima, Marchioness de Grey. It is often overlooked, being in a remote corner, but it has a picturesque setting and is supposed to look like a half ruined building, with great holes and rough arches on one side and a slightly neater thatched other half. A lovely folly.

The Archer pavilion excels in the French garden taste, but this bathhouse is its equal in the English style.

FLITTON

AN EMPTY CAP

Access:	Through village church. English Heritage, open weekends.
Map reference:	TL 059 359

Silsoe got its church only in 1831, and until then the parish church for Silsoe and the owners of **Wrest Park**, the De Grey family, was in Flitton. So the family mausoleum that the fifth Earl of Kent built for himself and his family started as a side chapel of Flitton's St John the Baptist church. The earliest monuments are visible from the church: the painted alabaster effigies of the builder Henry the Grey, who died in 1614, and his wife. Note their emblem in the top, a wyvern, the same winged monster that today crowns the Chinese Pavilion in Wrest Park.

The mausoleum was extended in 1705 into the shape of a cross by Henry de Grey, 12th Earl of Kent. All his seven children predeceased him and have memorials here. In 1710 he was made the first Duke of Kent by Queen Anne. That required more splendour in the gardens at Wrest Park (p.88) and an appropriately grand monument when he died in 1740. He is portrayed, probably by Rysbrack, in Roman attire, but with his hand on an English ducal cap. The cap is empty because there was no male heir to inherit it; he was succeeded by his favourite granddaughter Jemima, titled Marchioness de Grey.

One last flare of success for Wrest Park was the building of the present House by Thomas, Earl de Grey, and the enlarging of the gardens. This Thomas is seen in a huge Victorian-romantic relief, mourning his wife with his family.

It may be irreverent to say so, but we couldn't help noticing that this unique mausoleum is acoustically the best space in Bedfordshire for whistling.

HAYNES

LETTERS IN STONE

Access:	At Haynes Church End, 2 miles N of Clophill.
Map reference:	TL 082 411

We are fond of inscriptions. The mere fact that letters are carved into stone makes them deserve respect. Most inscriptions are found on churchyards. Often one finds someone's personal history, like the murder story of 'A Female Unknown' in **Tilsworth**, or the unspectacular confessions of vicar John Berridge at **Everton**. They may be simple texts, as the fast-fading one in **Bedford** for the mother of 24 children who died at 38 years of age, or even the one in **Luton** saying: 'Here lies the body of Thomas Procter - Who lived and died without a doctor'. Mausoleums usually carry texts, but none more explicitly so than the one for the Higgins family in the churchyard at **Turvey** (p.43). This mausoleum is three metres high and enormous stone letters are worked into the balustrade and shout: "What man is he that liveth and shall not see death?"

Only rarely does one find inscriptions on relatively normal houses like lodges. There is one in Haynes opposite the elaborate village pump and underneath the top floor with the remarkable iron sunflower finials. It runs round the house in four parts and is half Latin and half French:

DEO PATRIAE AMICIS - J'AYE BONNE CAUSE - LOYAL DEVOIR - FUTURUM INVISIBILE - ANNO DOMINI MDCCCLXXIII.

For God, country and friends - I have good reason - to do my duty faithfully - the future can't be seen - A D 1873.

CLOPHILL

THE HILL

Access: Where the High Street ends and the Shefford Road begins, a track to the left leads up to the church ruin.
Map reference: TL 092 389

Clophill has a few peculiarities. A lock-up and a pound for instance, side by side. Both are built in brickwork and oak, and they are in reasonably good condition. Further east in the High Street is St Mary's school, which has a little bell tower in its grounds: a relic from the old school and a source of inspiration for the pyramid roofs of the new.

Clophill's best curiosity is the fact that the old church is so far away from the village. Old St Mary's church is remarkable in that the north and south sides had only one window, albeit a large one. The ironstone church was originally right in the centre of the community, but the people moved downhill towards the road, probably on account of the Black Death. If so, the villagers built their church and immediately afterwards they made a fresh start elsewhere.

They continued to use the church and its graveyard however. The chancel was renewed in 1819. But soon after that they must have given up on it, since the new St Mary's church was built in 1848. The lovely old church on its hilltop perch looks romantic today. As such it makes a prettier picture than Someries chapel (p. 4, -**Luton**) or **Segenhoe** church. And it isn't lonely any more, for the place has been turned into a picnic area and there are new graves as well, nearby. It must be a pleasure lying there.

HIGHAM GOBION

A SAYING EXPLAINED?

> *Access:* One mile NE out of Barton-le-Clay.
> *Map reference: TL 104 328*

In Higham Gobion's church is a monument to Dr Castell (d. 1674), who was rector here and a professor of Arabic at Cambridge. He was quite an expert on Eastern languages, for he wrote one big, over-ambitious dictionary for seven of them, the *Lexicon Heptaglotton*. We could do with a few scholars like him, for nowadays it is even difficult for experts to agree on the meaning of the last two lines of this black plaque in the church. The fact that these last lines are in two languages, Latin and Arabic, and can be read as one sentence, may be said to tie in with his language skills.

The Latin part means: he chose to be buried here when he was still alive. The Arabic inscription, the earliest in Britain, is less simple. Being able to read Arabic is not the same as understanding what it says, apparently. Transposed in our letters the text reads from right to left: 'birajaa al madina afdal min tilk'. One person told us it meant that 'the people of Medina are the best'. But most Arabists we consulted seemed to agree that it meant something like: 'hoping for a better city than this one'.

Everyone said that 'madina' either means Medina (the city where Mohammed lies buried) or 'city', but never 'place' in general, which makes it mysterious. Taking the two lines together it could even be argued that Castell meant that while he lived here he wished he lived or was buried in Cambridge, instead of Higham Gobion!

PEGSDON

A SAYING EXPLAINED

Access:	Pub in village, just N of the B655.
Map reference:	TL 120 303

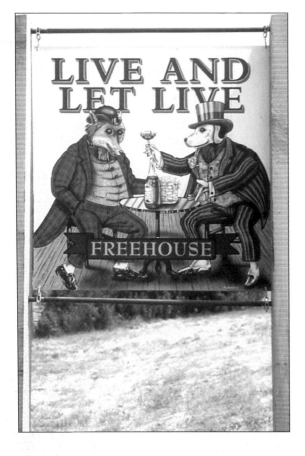

Most pubnames are easily explained. They usually derive from things like heraldry, religion, royalty, (local) celebrities, trades, animals and local features. But there is also a mixed bag, from which two pubs near **Barton-le-Clay** have taken a few. To the north is SPEED THE PLOUGH, to the east is LIVE AND LET LIVE.

In Pegsdon this latter name has given rise to several pubsigns to illustrate the motto. In the past there have been a Dog and Cat, a Tom and Jerry and a Fox and Chickens. But recently a new sign was put up following an idea of the new owners: the Fox and Hound.

According to local stories the pub's peculiar name was chosen almost 200 years ago, following a shoot-out between poachers and farmers, and after the shooting came the shouting and then, when it was clear that neither party could win, they all said, as local parlance has it: "Sod this, let's get drunk together". Which they did. Live and let live.

Other sources have it slightly differently. Apparently a police force from London set fire to straw piled against the walls of the pub, in order to smoke out a gang of poachers that were trapped inside. And maybe the landlord put in a good word for the leader of the gang, who was known as the Robin Hood of Hexton, and the men were spared. Not a bad story either. But we like the reconciliation story better. Don't you?

SHARPENHOE

NEEDLEWORK

Access:	Car park between Streatley and Sharpenhoe village.
Map reference: TL 066 302	

It has often been remarked that Bedfordshire can be seen as consisting of two main types of landscape: the chalk hills of the Chilterns in the south and the river landscape of the Ouse in the north. This is a simplification of course and anyone travelling through the county extensively will readily see that there is a surprising variety of lovely landscapes. Nevertheless it seems fitting to show at least two examples of curiosities that support this generalisation.

One is the old lock winding mechanisms at **Great Barford** (p.62), the other is the little obelisk on the Sharpenhoe Clappers. A grove of beech trees was planted on this chalk spur in the 19thC, but there were fortifications in the Iron Age already. It is all National Trust property now, presented by the man who also 'planted' an obelisk. It is 2.5 metres high, made of cement and gravel, and has a plaque, which tells of the death of two brothers during the Great War. Now you don't have to go and look for the obelisk itself, for it is not worth it. If there was a competition it would stand a good chance of getting the prize for the dullest little obelisk in England. However, the woods around here are good for a salubrious walk. The views are terrific, but are interrupted by trees and shrubs that grow on the slopes. There would be no harm in cutting a few of them. After all, it would be silly to have had a look-out point for centuries and then allow the view to be obstructed.

HARLINGTON

TREE AND STONE

Access:	From the E end of Harlington a footpath goes NE, down into Samshill / Samsell valley; the oaks stand alone.
Map reference:	TL 046 312

People who have read this book so far and know their Bedfordshire will sorely have missed mention of its most famous son John Bunyan. Here he is on the last page; he can't be avoided. His biography is too well-known to be repeated here. It can be picked up in many many places in the county which remind us of him and of his best-known book, *The Pilgrim's Progress*.

One of these places is what he calls the House Beautiful, the haunting ruin with the superb view: Houghton House near **Ampthill**. **Bedford** itself knows twelve such places (like the impressive bronze doors of the Bunyan Meeting Free Church), and **Elstow**, where he was born, five. There are two different John Bunyan Trails, footpaths of 25 and 45 miles, full of references.

For this book we have chosen Harlington and the two oaks. The Old Oak is supposed to be the tree under which Bunyan used to preach when he was in this area. He certainly was arrested and interrogated at Harlington Manor. The Old Oak died in the 1980s and some of its broken boughs were used to make an altar in the local church. A new oak was planted in 1988 to mark the tercentenary of Bunyan's death. For the next 300 years.

And Harlington has another curiosity: a mounting stone, to enable people to get on their horse easily. In front of the pub called 'the Carpenters Arms', which used to be a coach-

ing inn, it looks as if it is still used every day. While you are there, have a good look at the pubsign. Like some village signs, near the Moot Hall at **Elstow** for instance, there are two sides to it that are different.

Maybe they are symbolic for Bedfordshire: it is well worth a good look, and there is more to it than most English people realise.

INDEX

Pieter Boogaart was a teacher of English language and literature for twenty years. That was fine, but nowadays he reviews books for the Dutch libraries, which leaves him more time to nurse his rather severe case of Anglophilia.

Rita Boogaart is an art historian who recently left her job at the Open University in order to cooperate on projects like this book. She caught the English bug as well.

In the last thirty-'odd' years the Dutch couple have spent virtually all their holidays in Great Britain, looking for follies and curiosities. Ever since the Folly Fellowship was started they have been actively involved with it and contributed to its magazine.

Early in the year 2000 Pieter's book *A272 - An Ode to a Road* was published, a new type of cultural guidebook that he designed himself. It is about England as epitomised by this road in the south, and something on which they had worked together enthusiastically for five years.

In the picture Rita shows the curious hat, that she made for a special competition at the Folly Fellowship's Garden Party at Wrest Park in 1997. It was based on the roof of the Chinese Pavilion there (below and p. 67, 88) and it won her a bottle of wine.

Also published by **S. B. Publications** in the same series:

Curiosities of Berkshire

Curiosities of County Durham

Curiosities of Gloucestershire (The Cotswolds)

Curiosities of Gloucestershire (Severn Valley & Forest of Dean)

Secrets and Treasures of Northamptonshire

Curiosities of Oxfordshire

Curiosities of East Sussex

Curiosities of Wiltshire

S. B. Publications publish a wide range of local interest books covering aspects of local history, guides and walking books for many Counties in England.

For a free catalogue write to :-

S. B. Publications, 19 Grove Road, Seaford, East Sussex. BN25 1TP or access our website: **www.sbpublications.swinternet.co.uk**

NOTES